Ballads of American History

Written and produced by Fred Cooper
Sung by Gregg Harris

NOBLE PUBLISHING ASSOCIATES

P.O. BOX 2250

GRESHAM, OREGON 97030

(503) 667-3942

Ballads of American History
© 1996 by
Fred Cooper

An instrumental version of the enclosed Compact Disc is available by calling the publisher.

ISBN # 1-56857-033-3

Printed in the United States of America

PREFACE

As one grows older, the study and recollection of history becomes increasingly important to us. When we were young, we lacked that appreciation. In school, we often saw history as a "memory" course rather than as a study of those who had gone before us. We had a hard time understanding how decisions made by people of times past could have any bearing whatsoever on our lives in the present.

Ballads of American History was written in order to make the study of history more enjoyable and more memorable. While it is easy to forget facts which are merely learned for a test, we can generally remember songs we have learned in the past.

Producers of advertising know this fact better than anyone else. That's why they spend a fortune producing music and songs for their ads. When you think about it, you can easily recall the words of jingles you heard as a child as well as the words of songs you have learned since then.

The ballad, a musical form that has been around for many centuries, is simply a song that tells a story. Ballads had their origins in the twelfth century and were written to tell tales of great exploits, some mythical and some true. In the sixteenth century, troubadours went to country fairs in old England and sang ballads to earn a living. In addition to being entertaining, ballads were the way stories were handed down through generations.

Most modern songs have three or four verses and last two to three minutes leaving little room for content. A ballad, on the other hand, has many verses. Since the primary purpose is to tell a story, brevity of length is not the most important facet of composition.

The purpose of this book is not to present a full retelling of American History, but rather to explain the lyrics of the accompanying ballads on the tape or CD. In so doing, the book will give a fairly complete rendering of the subject covered by each song. These ballads are intended to supplement any standard book or course in American History.

When children learn the songs, they will remember the facts of specific historical periods. By learning the necessary facts about each historical event through music, that leaves time for asking the really important questions about each period—the "why" questions. These will stimulate the type of discussion and thinking for which the study of history was intended.

ACKNOWLEDGMENTS

I would like to thank several people whose help on this project has been extremely valuable. The music and the book were indeed a "family project." My wife, Sarah, is the true musician in our family and added greatly to the arrangement and preparation of the music. My son, Andy, helped with the lyrics and proofread the text. My younger son, Daniel, also assisted in proofreading the project and was a great encouragement to me. Our musical consultant, Diane Salo, provided much needed help with the arrangements. She composed the music for "The Plymouth Colony." Our friend and colleague, Linda Hurst, edited the text pointing out additional necessary information and helping to make it more readable for young readers. Gary D. Freeman, whose contribution to this project was invaluable, did all the orchestral arrangements and produced the musical tape. He played all the instrumental parts using the latest techniques in music synthesis. A very special word of thanks to Gregg Harris, my friend and publisher, who sang the songs and encouraged me in the process.

— Fred Cooper

FOREWORD

Perhaps one of the least appreciated parts of a child's education is the study of history. So often, history tests place such emphasis on names, places and dates that children miss out entirely on the great purposes of history. Instead of learning and understanding the great thoughts and ideas of the men and women who framed the events of history, they become bogged down in the memory work that will determine their grade in the course. Instead of retracing the motivations of yesterday's leaders, they fret over the spelling of their names. Instead of evaluating the achievements and mistakes of the past, they worry about tomorrow's homework deadline. Instead of learning the lessons from the past which might help avoid the mistakes of the future, they see history as the boring story of dead people from long ago.

It is necessary for students to learn a certain number of names, places, dates and events in order to evaluate history in its proper frame of reference. If that process could be made less painful, students could spend more time on those parts of history which will truly make them better stewards of the events of the present. That is the purpose of **Ballads of American History**.

These ballads help children learn the events of history in painless fashion. While no one enjoys the tedious memorization process, almost everyone loves a song. While we would rarely read facts from a book more than once, we enjoy hearing songs over and over again. That's one of the great values of music.

While these songs and the accompanying book are not intended to provide a comprehensive retelling and analysis of history, they do cover many of the great events about which students should know. If students could learn and understand the lyrics of these songs, they would have a much better framework of knowledge to evaluate the events of the past which so impact our lives today. In fact, if a student were to learn no more than the information in these songs, he would actually know more history than many adults today.

Hopefully, **Ballads of American History** will help students to learn and retain information which they will not easily forget for the years and years to come

— Dr. Richard Land

* Richard Land earned a P.h.D. from Oxford University and currently serves with the Southern Baptist Convention.

ROANOKE AND JAMESTOWN

About the music...
(Tape 1, Song 1)

The musical style of this ballad is folk music. If you have ever seen any movies about old England in the Fifteenth or Sixteenth Century, you may remember scenes from "country fairs." These were very much like county fairs today. There were musicians called **troubadours** (wandering minstrels who traveled from place to place). Maybe you have seen a "sidewalk musician" today who stands on a street corner and performs, placing a hat or basket by his side where people will drop money.

The instruments you hear are plucked stringed instruments similar to guitars today. You also hear flutes, cellos, and string basses which were common in that day. It is played in a "minor key." Music is written in a minor key when it describes something that is sad, or doleful. Such themes as the Lost Roanoke Colony and the sufferings of Jamestown are best expressed in this way.

Queen Elizabeth sought for English pride.
She wanted for her country a colony to guide.
They knew about the New World in that land across the sea.
That land we call America, uncivilized but free.

Sir Walter Raleigh planned that colony abroad;
The queen gave him a charter to rule that foreign sod.
He hired two sea captains who Roanoke Island claimed.
In honor of their good queen, Virginia, it was named.

Chorus

They came from England, across the stormy sea,
They came to found a new land for you and me.

In 1585, they took one hundred men
To found on Roanoke Island the colony for them.
The men sought gold and fortune rather than to tame the land,
But the project failed and they returned to England once again.

Two years later, Sir Walter tried once more.
  He sent a group of families to settle this new shore.
To found such a colony was dangerous indeed.
  These people had commitment, a tough and noble breed.

Chorus

Back to England went the governor because he realized
  Their project soon would fail unless they had some new supplies.
But England was involved in a great sea war with Spain.
  For three long years, in England did the governor remain.

The English governor returned to take his place.
  But found that the settlers disappeared without a trace.
They sent several ships who did seek and search in vain.
  But the lost Roanoke colony was never found again.

Chorus

Twenty long years later, King James was on the throne.
  He thought once more the New World was for Englishmen to own.
There was a group of merchants called the London Company
  Who hired ships and men to once more cross the stormy sea.

The king sought for a passage to India by sea.
  He hoped for gold and riches to flow continuously.
To find the Lost Colony of Roanoke was their hope.
  Also, to spread the gospel to all the native folk.

Chorus

In choosing new colonists to make the trip succeed,
  Half were wealthy gentlemen who'd never worked indeed.
They thought that gold and fortune soon would quickly come their way.
  Then they'd return to England far richer men one day.

In Sixteen Seven, they came in vessels three.
  They entered the James River to found their colony.
They chose their land unwisely near a swamp where varmints thrive.
  Mosquitoes and diseases took their toll of human lives.

Chorus

Captain John Smith was the man who took control.
　　He forced the Jamestown colonists, each man to pull his load.
When one day he was injured, to England he returned.
　　Starvation took its toll when idle men their work did spurn.

Of those five hundred men who tried to make the project thrive.
　　Only sixty souls the hardships did survive.
As they started back to England, they were greeted by new men.
　　So, they returned and settled little Jamestown once again.

Chorus

They began their work again under leadership anew.
　　Slowly, through hard work a new success they did pursue.
When, in 1619, ninety women did arrive,
　　They married Englishmen and with families they did thrive.

Tobacco was the crop which brought the pay they long had sought.
　　They finally realized their search for gold was all for naught.
But the greatest wealth of Jamestown in that World across the sea
　　Was the chance to build a life in a land that would be free.

Chorus

Ship Arriving at Jamestown

Roanoke and Jamestown

"He that will not work shall not eat, except by sickness he be disabled."
-Captain John Smith

The Discovery and Early Exploration of America

Christopher Columbus discovered America in 1492. Though the northern parts of the continent had actually been visited by the **Vikings** 500 years earlier, it was the discovery by Columbus that caused men of many countries to begin exploration of this land.

At first, Columbus thought he had reached India. Neither he nor anyone else at that time knew of the existence of what we now call North and South America. Many other sea captains made voyages to the land they thought to be part of India. In 1497, an English map maker named **John Cabot** sailed a course farther north than that of Columbus and discovered North America. He claimed that land for England.

Another explorer, an Italian named **Amerigo Vespucci**, discovered what is now South America, and he called it the **New World**. The Europeans actually thought that Columbus and Vespucci had discovered two different lands. In 1507, the new world was named after Amerigo Vespucci. Even though the people of Europe later realized that Columbus had actually discovered the new world first, the name America was already established in men's minds.

In the 1500's, the Spaniards did much exploration of South America and Mexico. They even ventured into what is now the American West. One Spanish explorer, **Hernando De Soto**, landed in Florida and explored what is now Alabama and Mississippi. But no permanent settlement was established at that time. During the same time period, the French landed in Canada.

More than 100 years after John Cabot claimed the North American continent for England the first permanent English settlement in what is now the United States was undertaken by the English. By 1565, the Spaniards had built a permanent settlement in St. Augustine, Florida.

Amerigo Vespucci

Roanoke and Jamestown

Queen Elizabeth sought for English pride.
> *She wanted for her country a colony to guide.*
They knew about the New World in that land across the sea.
> *That land we call America, uncivilized but free.*

Sir Walter Raleigh planned that colony abroad;
> *The queen gave him a charter to rule that foreign sod.*
He hired two sea captains who Roanoke Island claimed,
> *In honor of their good queen, Virginia, it was named.*

Chorus

They came from England, across the stormy sea.
> *They came to found a new land for you and me.*

Queen Elizabeth was the ruler of England in 1585. Like most rulers, she wanted her country to have great conquests in the world. When her good friend, **Sir Walter Raleigh,** asked for permission to establish a colony in the New World, she was very happy to grant him a **charter,** a document granting permission to establish a settlement and rule a certain piece of land. Since the English believed the land belonged to them, the Queen was the ruler of the land. Without a charter, a person had no authority to rule in that land. The Queen needed the advice of Sir Walter for the many important decisions that England faced, so she did not allow him to go personally to America. He hired the captains and the men who made the dangerous voyage. When the English arrived in America, they discovered an island that the Indians called **Roanoke**. They chose the island for their settlement because it gave them good protection from unfriendly Indians. They named the mainland next to the island "Virginia" to honor Queen Elizabeth, who was called the "Virgin Queen."

Queen Elizabeth

In 1585, they took one hundred men
  To found on Roanoke Island the colony for them.
The men sought gold and fortune rather than to tame the land,
  But the project failed and they returned to England once again.

What type of men would agree to go to a new land? Just think! There would be none of the conveniences of life in England—no shops or markets for food and products they used every day, no army or police force for protection, no doctors to treat them if they became ill, and certainly no instant communication with people in England. The ocean voyage alone was extremely dangerous. A man would need a very good reason to take so great a risk. The men who made the voyage were men who thought they would gain great wealth. Some had heard rumors that the beaches were strewn with large gold nuggets just waiting to be picked up like ripe plums from a tree. They did not realize how dangerous the wilderness of America was with its fierce Indians. They did not comprehend the danger of diseases harbored by insects in the swampy coastlines of Virginia and Carolina. When they arrived, they immediately began to look for gold and silver and paid little attention to the essential task of planting gardens to raise food for the months ahead. For this reason, they ran out of food and supplies. They also had hostile confrontations with the Indians. They soon had to pack up and return to England in failure.

Two years later, Sir Walter tried once more.
  He sent a group of families to settle this new shore.
To found such a colony was dangerous indeed.
  These people had commitment, a tough and noble breed.

Back to England went the governor because he realized
  Their project soon would fail unless they had some new supplies.
But England was involved in a great sea war with Spain.
  For three long years, in England did the governor remain.

The English governor returned to take his place.
  But found that the settlers disappeared without a trace.
They sent several ships who did seek and search in vain.
  But the lost Roanoke colony was never found again.

Still wanting to succeed, Sir Walter Raleigh decided to hire a different type of people to settle the land. Instead of hiring men who wanted only wealth and adventure, he selected families to make the journey, thinking they would be more willing to build homes, establish farms and truly settle the land. This

Sir Walter Raleigh

group of people departed for America in 1587 and settled the original colony on Roanoke Island. When the supplies brought from England began to run low, the Governor, John White, decided to return to England to obtain new supplies. Before departing, he gave instructions to the colonists to carve a message on a certain tree if they were to leave the island. Also, if they were in trouble, they were to carve a cross on the tree.

When Governor White arrived in England, he learned that England was at war with Spain. Every ship was needed for the great naval battle that was to take place, so he could not return to England until the war was over, regardless of the needs of those families in America. When, after three long years, he was able to obtain a ship to return to Roanoke, he found no one there. On the tree was carved the word, "Croatoan," the name of another island in the area. He searched in vain and did not find even a trace or clue of the whereabouts of the colonists. Sir Walter Raleigh sent other search expeditions, but the people were never found. That is why the colony has always been called **"The Lost Colony."** People then realized how dangerous the task of colonization actually was. Twenty years passed before the English were willing to try again.

> *Twenty long years later, King James was on the throne.*
> *He thought once more the New World was for Englishmen to own.*
> *There was a group of merchants called the London Company*
> *Who hired ships and men to once more cross the stormy sea.*
>
> *The king sought for a passage to India by sea.*
> *He hoped for gold and riches to flow continuously,*
> *To find the Lost Colony of Roanoke was their hope*
> *Also, to spread the gospel to all the native folk.*

Queen Elizabeth died and was succeeded on the throne by **King James I**. (If you have ever heard of the King James Version of the Bible, this is the king after whom that is named. He wanted men to read the Bible in the English language). One of his objectives was to spread the Christian faith to America.

Actually, the king had four reasons for wanting to establish a colony in America:

1. To find a river or sea route across America which would lead to India.

2. To spread the Christian faith to the Indians of America.

3. To find gold and other wealth.

4. To find some remnant of the Lost Colony of Roanoke.

Such an expedition was very, very costly. Rather than using money from the treasury, he allowed the project to be financed by a group of wealthy merchants who banded together to form a company called **The London Company**. The company paid the cost of hiring the ships. They also paid for all the food and supplies that would be needed for the journey and the early days of colonization. The men who made the journey were to pay back The London Company with goods from the New World such as furs, lumber, agricultural products and, hopefully, gold which might be discovered. If the colonists should discover a sea route to India, the London Company stood to become very wealthy. Unfortunately, though, they had no idea how vast the land of America was and how enormous the great ocean which separated America from the Far East was.

> *In choosing new colonists to make the trip succeed,*
> *Half were wealthy gentlemen who'd never worked indeed.*
> *They thought that gold and fortune soon would quickly come their way.*
> *Then they'd return to England far richer men one day.*

Again, a choice of people to travel to America had to be made. How would you choose people for this project? Chances are, you would choose men from various trades; farmers, fishermen, carpenters, stone masons, blacksmiths, etc. who could work as a team to accomplish the many tasks that would be required in establishing and running a successful community. Unfortunately, about half of those who made the trip were wealthy gentlemen from the upper classes who had never done manual labor. These men were adventurers who thought they would easily find gold which would bring them instant riches.

Today, almost everyone works at a job of some kind. In those days, however, society had distinct divisions between nobility, or upper class, and the lower classes of people. Members of the nobility did not do the types of work that commoners did.

> *In Sixteen Seven, they came in vessels three.*
> *They entered the James River to found their colony.*
> *They chose their land unwisely near a swamp where varmints thrive.*
> *Mosquitoes and diseases took their toll of human lives.*

On May 6, 1607, the adventurers, 105 in number, arrived off the coast of Virginia in three ships: **The Susan Constant**, the **Godspeed**, and the **Discovery**. They discovered the mouth of a river which they named the **James River** after King James. About 60 miles upstream, they established their settlement on a little peninsula of the river and named it **Jamestown**, also after their king. But, again, they chose unwisely! The land was swampy and full of mosquitoes and other varmints. Over half the men died of malnutrition and diseases such as malaria, pneumonia and dysentery.

> *Captain John Smith was the man who took control.*
>   *He forced the Jamestown colonists, each man to pull his load.*
> *When one day he was injured, to England he returned.*
>   *Starvation took its toll when idle men their work did spurn.*

The lazy, gold-seeking gentlemen did not plant gardens and raise the food they would need to survive. Instead, they sought their fortunes in vain. When the first winter arrived, there was not enough food for everyone. The settlers faced great hardships. The main problem the men faced was a lack of leadership. About a year after the colony was established, a good leader named **Captain John Smith** took control and ruled with a heavy hand. He dictated that if a man would not work, he would not eat, and stood by his word. The colony began to function successfully under his leadership. He was able to command the respect of the colonists and to establish trade with the Indians.

> *Of those five hundred men who tried to make the project thrive.*
>   *Only sixty souls the hardships did survive.*
> *As they started back to England, they were greeted by new men.*
>   *So, they returned and settled little Jamestown once again.*

Unfortunately, in 1609, Smith was injured in an accident and had to return to England. Again, the colony suffered from a lack of strong leadership, and the wealthy refused to work. By the time Captain Smith left for England, the colony had grown to a population of 500. During the winter of 1609-1610, which was called **"the starving time,"** all but 60 of the colonists died of starvation and disease. Those sixty, in their weakened condition, had decided to return to England, and on their way down the James River toward the ocean, were met by a ship bringing new settlers and supplies. The sixty returned and re-established the colony. Under the strong leadership of **Governor Thomas West,** whose title was **Lord De La Warr**, the colony was saved. (The State of Delaware was later named after this man.)

> *They began their work again under leadership anew.*
>   *Slowly, through hard work a new success they did pursue.*
> *When, in 1619, ninety women did arrive,*
>   *They married Englishmen and with families they did thrive.*
>
> *Tobacco was the crop which brought the pay they long had sought.*
>   *They finally realized their search for gold was all for naught.*
> *But the greatest wealth of Jamestown in that World across the sea*
>   *Was the chance to build a life in a land that would be free.*

Surveying the new land

After the colony was re-established in 1610, they began to plant corn and raise hogs on their farms. But their greatest success was in the development of tobacco, a money crop which could be exported.

Most of the colonists in those early years were men. In 1619, the London Company sent 90 women to Jamestown to marry and establish families. This gave the men new purpose in life, and the colony became permanently established.

Sadly, another group arrived that same year. A group of black slaves was brought ashore. Slavery was established in America from the very beginning. Little did they know at that time the terrible problems the new nation would face in future years because of the evil institution of slavery.

Nonetheless, the success of Jamestown drew other Englishmen and Europeans to America in future years and made possible the eventual formation of the United States of America.

Study Questions:

1. Why do you think Queen Elizabeth wanted to own colonies in the New World?

2. What might have motivated a person to make the dangerous voyage across the Atlantic to the New World?

3. It seems that the colonists of Jamestown had a hard time providing for themselves in the wilderness. Why were the Englishmen so totally unprepared for life in America?

4. If you were a member of Chief Powhatan's tribe (the tribe which inhabited Virginia) in those days, how would you have felt toward the English?

5. Do you think the English were wrong in desiring to come to America?

6. Do you think Europeans had a right to come to America?

7. Do you think the Indians had a right to try to drive the Englishmen from the land?

London Company sent 90 women to Jamestown to marry and establish families.

Delfthaven, Holland

THE PLYMOUTH COLONY

About the music...
(Tape 1, Song 2)

The music for this ballad is done in a style similar to what would be heard in a church. If you were to visit a great old cathedral in England or anywhere else in Europe, you would hear music from great pipe organs. They were able to build such great instruments even one thousand years ago. For that matter, the Romans had similar instruments two thousand years ago.

Since the Pilgrims were a religious people who traveled to America for religious reasons, this style of music was used. It is similar to the type of psalms they would have sung in their worship. Because they were unable to bring a pipe organ with them, the Pilgrims sang a capella (voices only).

In addition to the organ, you hear drums which are used at points of emphasis as the music becomes more exciting. The song is played in a major key to express a happy or positive theme. In this case, it expresses the triumph of the Pilgrims in spite of the difficulties they faced. It underscores the victory of faith over all obstacles.

In 1600, King James did reign.
    He ruled all England and its vast domain.
The Church of England did the king sustain,
    But other churches did he thus restrain.

Many people in that day did try
    The Church of England, then, to purify.
The state religion did not satisfy.
    Their faith in God they would not deny.

Chorus

The Pilgrims suffered in those early years.
    Their faith sustained them through their toil and tears.

King James resisted with a heavy hand,
　　Imprisoned Puritans throughout the land
The persecution did their faith expand.
　　Their dedication was a thing so grand.

The king's fierce anger they could not ignore.
　　They fled for safety o'er to Holland's shore.
Religious freedom did they find in store,
　　But with Dutch culture they had no rapport.

Chorus

The New World was a place where they could go
　　Where seeds of faith and life could freely grow.
The king, a charter he did then bestow.
　　The winds of freedom, then, would surely blow.

These hardy Pilgrims did one day set sail,
　　One hundred Englishmen who would not fail.
Their six week journey filled with great travail,
　　Through many hardships would they then prevail.

Chorus

To sail to Jamestown was their first intent,
　　But stormy weather just would not relent.
So far from Virginia, the Mayflower went
　　To northern reaches of the continent.

In 1620 did the Lord provide.
　　Off Plymouth's shore the Pilgrims did arrive.
They set a village in the countryside
　　Just two short days before the Christmastide.

Chorus

The land was north of England's sure domain.
　　There were no rulers on this new terrain.
The Mayflower Compact did their law contain;
　　So law and order in the land would reign.

That first long winter there were hardships great.
　　The food supply could not accommodate.
Disease did half their number decimate;
　　Their courage, one could never overstate.

Chorus

In springtime, Samoset and Squanto came;
>   They taught them how to farm and capture game.
The Indians their lasting friends became;
>   A friendship covenant did the men proclaim.

The autumn brought abundant harvesting;
>   To God their words of praise and thanks did ring.
The Indians joined this happy gathering.
>   They shared a feast we now call Thanksgiving.

Chorus

The Mayflower-Plymouth Settlement

The Pilgrims of Plymouth Colony

"We are well weaned from the delicate milk of our mother country, and inured to the difficulties of a strange and hard land, which yet in a great part we have by patience overcome....It is not with us as with other men, whom small things can discourage, or small discontentments cause to wish themselves at home again."

> - William Brewster and John Robinson, leaders of the Plymouth Colony, in a letter applying for financing for their voyage to America.

In 1600, King James did reign.
He ruled all England and its vast domain.
The Church of England did the king sustain,
But other churches did he thus restrain.

The Pilgrims suffered in those early years.
Their faith sustained them through their toil and tears.

King James I was the same king who gave the charter to establish the Jamestown Colony in 1607. As king, he was head of the **Church of England**, also, now known as the **Anglican Church** or the **Episcopal Church**. He believed all people must belong to that church only and would not allow the existence of other Christian churches. In fact, he became a persecutor of those who, because of their conscientious beliefs, decided to leave the Church of England.

Many people in that day did try
The Church of England, then, to purify.
The state religion did not satisfy.
Their faith in God they would not deny.

King James resisted with a heavy hand,
Imprisoned Puritans throughout the land
The persecution did their faith expand.
Their dedication was a thing so grand.

There were several groups who believed the Church of England had become corrupt. They saw that the religion practiced in many of the churches was merely a formality. Many of the ministers were only interested in the prestige and money that came from the ministry, as the church was financially supported by the government of England. These groups believed the practice of true and undefiled religion was becoming non-existent in that government-sponsored church.

The Plymouth Colony

Some sincere groups of people tried to work within the church to bring reform. These people were called **Puritans** because they wanted to "purify" the church. Others left the church and formed new churches. These people were called **Separatists**. When the King and his men discovered the secret meetings of these people, they persecuted them, throwing them into prisons.

The king's fierce anger they could not ignore.
They fled for safety o'er to Holland's shore.
Religious freedom did they find in store,
But with Dutch culture they had no rapport.

Unable to function under the heavy hand of King James, the Separatists decided to leave England. They had heard that in Holland, there was complete religious freedom, that they could establish their own community in that country and worship as they pleased without persecution. Since their faith in God and the devout practice of their religion was the most important part of their lives, they decided to flee England. The King's government was not willing to let them go, even though they were few in number. However, under great hardship, they were able to escape England and establish their community in Holland. But even there, the agents of King James sought to persecute them.

While they did enjoy religious freedom in Holland, they were still Englishmen and loved the ways and culture of their native land. Their children were losing their English heritage and were becoming like Dutchmen. This was more than they could bear. Also, they were considered to be second class citizens in Holland since most could not afford to buy land or go into the better paying skilled trades. They truly wanted to return in peace to England. However, this was not possible.

The New World was a place where they could go
Where seeds of faith and life could freely grow.
The king, a charter he did then bestow.
The winds of freedom, then, would surely blow.

By about 1615, they had heard of Jamestown and the success of the colony in the New World. The king had bestowed a charter to the Virginia Company. Settling in Virginia appealed the Pilgrims, and they were granted a charter by the Virginia Company to settle in America.

A Native American

These hardy Pilgrims did one day set sail,
One hundred Englishmen who would not fail.
Their six week journey filled with great travail,
Through many hardships would they then prevail.

In 1620, two ships, the **Speedwell** and the **Mayflower** set sail from England for Virginia. The Speedwell began to take on water, and the ships had to return to England. The group of 102 passengers then crowded onto the Mayflower. They included 41 Separatists and 61 other Englishmen who, though they were not part of their religious group, wanted to go to the New World.

> *To sail to Jamestown was their first intent,*
> *But stormy weather just would not relent.*
> *So far from Virginia, the Mayflower went*
> *To northern reaches of the continent.*

Any journey across the Atlantic in those days was very dangerous. There was a good chance of death from shipwreck or disease. Would you have been willing to take such a chance as this? People who were willing to take this risk had to have a very good reason for doing so. The journey was particularly dangerous in the fall of the year. The Pilgrims felt, however, that when they arrived in Virginia, the colonists who had gone before them would be able to help them get a start in the new land.

The Pilgrims wanted to settle somewhere north of Jamestown which, of course, was the only settled place in Virginia. Virginia was much larger than the state we know today. It extended as far north as the mouth of the Hudson River (present day New York City). Perhaps they wanted to settle somewhere in that northern area of the colony where they might have access to Jamestown, but be far enough away that their differences would not be a problem. The reference to the Jamestown destination properly refers to the area north of Jamestown, where a good site for their colony might have existed.

Their mission did not work out as they had planned, however. Storms in the North Atlantic tossed the little ship off course. The journey took six weeks, and they ultimately arrived hundreds of miles north of their intended destination near Cape Cod, Massachusetts. The place where they arrived was called Plymouth. It had been given that name earlier in 1612 by Captain John Smith, the man who had ruled at the Jamestown Colony.

> *In 1620 did the Lord provide.*
> *Off Plymouth's shore the Pilgrims did arrive.*
> *They set a village in the countryside*
> *Just four short days before the Christmastide.*
>
> *The land was north of England's sure domain.*
> *There were no rulers on this new terrain.*
> *The Mayflower Compact did their law contain;*
> *So law and order in the land would reign.*

The Landing of the Pilgrims

The master of the ship knew they had arrived at Cape Cod. Even though the English had not settled the area, the land had been mapped out and identified by earlier explorers. They decided to settle in that area rather than to sail for Virginia. The group knew that without the authority of an organized government, men could not live in peace and civility. Therefore, the men gathered in the cabin of the Mayflower and wrote a document which came to be called **The Mayflower Compact**. In this famous document, they pledged to establish an organized local government to which they would subject themselves. This was not a separate national government, however. They still considered themselves to be Englishmen under the authority of the King.

The Pilgrims did not immediately go ashore. First, they had to explore the land to see if it would be safe to leave the ship. They knew there were hostile Indians in the new land. They took their time. In fact, the Pilgrims continued to live on the ship for a month before they made the final decision for all to go ashore. During that time, the men scouted out the land and selected a location for the colony which would offer good protection from the Indians, an adequate water supply and good land for farming.

> *That first long winter there were hardships great.*
> *The food supply could not accommodate.*
> *Disease did half their number decimate;*
> *Their courage, one could never overstate.*

They went ashore just before Christmas in 1620. That first winter was a tragic and difficult one, indeed, so much so that half the Pilgrims died of disease. Though the food supply brought from England was limited, the Pilgrims did not die of starvation. They survived on what supplies they had on the ship and on the shellfish which they could gather from the sands of the seashore.

> *In springtime, Samoset and Squanto came;*
> *They taught them how to farm and capture game;*
> *The Indians their lasting friends became.*
> *A friendship covenant did the men proclaim.*

After that first sad winter, the Pilgrims were greatly blessed during the first springtime with some very fortunate events. One day, the colonists saw an Indian approaching their little fortified village. They were terrified. They grasped their guns nervously fearing an attack. How surprised they were to hear this man speak to them in English. Though no colony had been established, English fishermen had ventured into the land and had established trade with the Indians. Many of them, like this man named **Samoset**, learned to speak some English. How much more astonished they were to learn that Samoset knew of another Indian man who had actually lived in England and who spoke fluent English. This man, named **Squanto,** had been kidnapped several years earlier and, through a series of events, ended up in England. He had returned to the New World on a trading ship only to find that his tribe had been wiped out by an epidemic. He felt comfortable with the English and went to live with them. Through these friendly Indians, they established a long-lasting friendship with **Massasoit**, the principal chief of the Indians of that region. Squanto also taught them the methods of farming practiced by the Indians which would be successful in that land.

> *The autumn brought abundant harvesting;*
> *To God their words of praise and thanks did ring.*
> *The Indians joined this happy gathering.*
> *They shared a feast we now call Thanksgiving.*

1st Thanksgiving – 1621 Harvest Feast

After planting fields in the spring with the help of their Indian friends, and after establishing friendly relations with the tribes of the area, the seeds of success were planted. They also learned the hunting and fishing methods of the Indians which would serve them well for the future in this great wilderness land. In 1821, they had a great three-day feast to which they invited their Indian friends. This was a time of great celebration and thanksgiving to God. They established that great tradition which came to be known as "Thanksgiving." That is one reason why that little colony came to be remembered so prominently in the history of the United States.

Study Questions:

1. Why do you think the Pilgrim Separatists wanted to leave England? Could you think of any conditions that would cause you to consider leaving your country?

2. Do you think the Separatists decided correctly in choosing to leave England for Holland? What alternatives did they have? What would you have chosen to do in those circumstances?

3. Why do you think the Pilgrims chose to come to America from Holland rather than return to England?

4. When the Mayflower arrived in New England, they knew they were off course. Why do you think they chose to stay in New England rather than going to Virginia as they had originally intended?

5. Suppose you were the leader of the Pilgrims and you had just landed on the coast of New England. Would you have chosen to have the ship sail hundreds of miles to Virginia or to found the new colony in the unknown land of New England?

6. Like the settlers of Virginia, the Pilgrims also seemed rather unprepared for settling in the New World. How could they have better prepared themselves for settling in an uncivilized land?

7. What do you think enabled the Pilgrims to survive after having lost half their number to disease and deprivation in the wilderness of Plymouth?

8. What lessons have you learned from the study of the Plymouth Colony?

Early Settlers in Virginia

THE THIRTEEN COLONIES IN AMERICA

About the music...
(Tape 1, Song 3)

This is a semi-classical type of music using the standard orchestra instruments you commonly hear today. It is done in a cheerful major key to portray the cheerful theme.

Just after 1600, to America there came,
    Courageous folk from Europe whose spirits were aflame.
Some came to worship freely, others sought for fortunes grand.
    But all sought for a new life in this large and untamed land.

Virginia was the first one; by Englishmen 'twas formed.
    These men had heard that gold and fortune lay for them in store.
They came in 1607; many men did not survive.
    Tobacco brought the wealth that gold and silver had denied.

Chorus

The colonies were formed by both the humble and the great
    And from these thirteen colonies, they formed the United States.

The colony of Georgia was first claimed by France and Spain.
    In 1629, a group of English merchants came.
In 17 and 30, it was named for good King George.
    'Twas prisoners and debtors, the first lasting township forged.

In the 1500's was South Carolina claimed
    By unsuccessful settlers from the land of Spain.
King Charles of old England in 1633,
    Did grant the land to Englishmen who settled there indeed.

Chorus

North Carolina's early story was the same.
    In 17 and 12, the land got its new name.
German and Swiss settlers were the first ones in the land,
    But King Charles of Great Britain did later take command.

The Swedish and the Dutchmen first settled Delaware.
  But the English won New Netherlands to Holland's great despair.
It soon became a part of Pennsylvania, and then,
  In 1704, it separated once again.

Chorus

Maryland was for the Virgin Mary surely named.
  For Roman Catholic settlers, church freedom was obtained,
But much religious fighting continued through the years.
  The king appointed governors, the colony to steer.

New Jersey was discovered back in 1524.
  One hundred years thereafter, Swedes and Dutchmen came ashore.
The Englishmen then conquered Dutch possessions in the land.
  Religious freedom reigned when Quaker owners took their stand.

Chorus

The French and the Dutch both occupied New York,
  But English armies took control in 1664.
The Dutch and English trappers with the Indians did trade,
  But French and English wars, the white men's settlement delayed.

The Puritans and Pilgrims settled Massachusetts' shores.
  They sought religious freedom from their British overlords.
They were friendly with the Indians who helped them to survive,
  But over foreign politics with the English they did strive.

Chorus

The settlers of Connecticut from Massachusetts came.
  Founded small religious colonies in their churches' names.
They wanted independence from the King of England's laws.
  They were among the first to speak their mind in freedom's cause.

Those who formed Rhode Island came from Massachusetts, too,
  To practice their religion without government ado.
The land was rich and fertile, their ports were hubs of trade.
  Independent church and state foundations there were laid.

Chorus

New Hampshire was established by decision of King James.
    Two English noblemen were given major land domains.
At first, it was a part of Massachusetts colony.
    The king, the land divided so they'd function separately.

King James gave a charter to a man named William Penn,
    A land once owned by Sweden and the Netherlands.
The Quakers for religious freedom ventured to this land.
    They were first to place the government in the people's hands.

Chorus

These colonies, at first, behaved like independent states,
    But all were ruled by England through the monarch's designates.
Some were loyal to the king, while others soon rebelled.
    One day they got together; a new nation they beheld.

Chorus

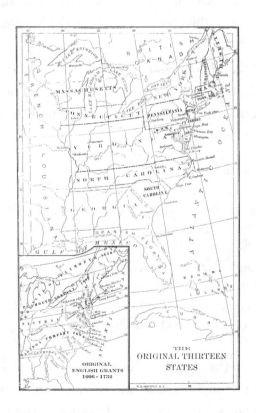

The Thirteen Colonies in America

"Yesterday, the greatest question was decided which ever was debated in America, and a greater perhaps never was nor will be decided among men. A resolution was passed without one dissenting colony, 'that these United Colonies are, and of right ought to be, free and independent States.'"
-John Adams in a letter to his wife, Abigail Adams, July 3, 1776.

The **Norsemen** came to America about 1,000 A.D. These were men from the lands of Northern Europe such as current day Norway, Denmark and Sweden. Their discovery of this hemisphere did not cause much stir in the world. Neither did they try to establish permanent colonies. Christopher Columbus came in 1492. Over the next century, explorers from European countries came to both North and South America. During the 16th century, the Spaniards began to occupy what is now called Latin America.

The North American continent was occupied by Indians of many tribes, peoples whose ways of life were quite different from the Europeans who had to come to this New World.

But the Europeans came, first by the hundreds, then by the thousands to establish beachheads in the wilderness which became colonies. These colonies then became the states,which united to form our country.

Why did they come? What motivated them to leave their homes, families, and way of life in Europe to journey to a new, undeveloped place with none of the conveniences of European culture? The chance of dying on the journey across the Atlantic in a sailing ship was significant. Survival in the wilderness of America was also very difficult.

> *Just after 1600, to America there came,*
> *Courageous folk from Europe whose spirits were aflame.*
> *Some came to worship freely, others sought for fortunes grand.*
> *But all sought for a new life in this large and untamed land.*
>
> *Virginia was the first one; by Englishmen 'twas formed.*
> *These men had heard that gold and fortune lay for them in store.*
> *They came in 1607; many men did not survive.*
> *Tobacco brought the wealth that gold and silver had denied.*

The first permanent settlement in the original thirteen colonies was Jamestown. Though an attempt was made to settle in Virginia in 1585, that was unsuccessful. The families who formed the Roanoke Colony disappeared without a trace. It became known as "The Lost Colony." About twenty years later, England tried again. Tragically, most of the original colonists died of starvation or disease, but the colony itself survived and grew.

Those who made that journey were motivated by the desire to find riches. They had heard that gold and silver were abundant and easy to find. While there were a few missionaries among those settlers, Virginia was not a religious colony as were many of the others. They did not find wealth in gold or silver. They eventually gained profits from farming the land. The big money crop was tobacco, particularly the new types of tobacco developed in Virginia.

> The colony of Georgia was first claimed by France and Spain.
> In 1629, a group of English merchants came.
> In 17 and 30, it was named for good King George.
> 'Twas prisoners and debtors, the first lasting township forged.

The famous explorer, Fernando de Soto, was probably the first European to set foot on Georgia. It was the French, however, who established the first colony there about 1564, more than twenty years before Englishmen ever settled in America. The French and the Spaniards fought over that first settlement, and it did not continue. No one really settled in Georgia for many years.

In 1629, the English claimed the land for themselves. But even they did not occupy the area until 100 years later. Though it was one of the first areas to be explored, Georgia was actually the last of the thirteen original colonies to be established by England.

It was established for a very interesting purpose. A man named **James Oglethorpe** wanted to establish a place in America for poor people who had been cast into prison in England because they could not find employment. These people had not committed crimes, but were put in prison because they could not pay their debts. Georgia was to be a place where they could start a new life, a place where there would be a vast amount of land to be farmed and developed.

The land was undeveloped. The king also knew that if England did not occupy that land, the Spaniards in Florida would take control of the area.

> In the 1500's was South Carolina claimed
>   By unsuccessful settlers from the land of Spain.
> King Charles of old England in 1633,
>   Did grant the land to Englishmen who settled there indeed.

James Oglethrope

While the Spaniards were the first to come to the land now known as South Carolina, they were not successful in keeping a colony there. After the English settled Virginia, the first Englishmen began to move to the land south of their colony.

Since the land was claimed by England, the king actually owned the land. He had the right to give it to anyone he wished. King Charles gave a charter to eight noblemen who desired to make money from the land. In 1633 they named the land after King Charles, hence the name "Carolina." The first town was called Charles Town, later changed to Charleston. At first, there was no such division as North Carolina or South Carolina. The original eight men to whom the charter was given did not rule well. They also angered the Indians. After many years, they sold the land back to the king. The settlers were displeased and rebelled against these men.

King Charles

> *North Carolina's early story was the same.*
> *In 17 and 12, the land got its new name.*
> *German and Swiss settlers were the first ones in the land,*
> *But King Charles of Great Britain did later take command.*

Prior to the time when Carolina was divided into North and South Carolina, German and Swiss settlers also came to the land and established a colony called **New Bern**. However, that colony was destroyed in a war with the Indians.

It was the King of England who divided Carolina into two separate lands which came to be called North Carolina and South Carolina. He appointed a governor to rule over each. South Carolina became wealthier by developing money crops such as rice and cotton. Unfortunately, they bought African slaves to work the land. That is why South Carolina was able to develop its wealth more quickly. The people who moved to North Carolina were not wealthy enough to own slaves, so they worked the land themselves.

> *The Swedish and the Dutchmen first settled Delaware.*
> *But the English won New Netherlands to Holland's great despair.*
> *It soon became a part of Pennsylvania, and then,*
> *In 1704, it separated once again.*

Henry Hudson

Dutchmen were the first to come to the land we know as Delaware. However, they did not get along with the Indians, and their settlement failed. The Swedes then sent a group of settlers to establish a colony which they called **New Sweden**. They had friendly relations with the Indians, and their colony survived. Unfortunately, though, Sweden was not able to provide financial support for the colony, and few settlers actually came over. The land was taken over by the Dutch in 1655. Just ten years later, the British, who were already well established in America, took control of the colony. In 1682, the Duke of York gave Delaware to Willian Penn to become part of his Pennsylvania colony so that Pennsylvania could have a connection to the ocean. In 1704 the people in these counties which comprised Delaware asked that they be granted a separate legislature. Their request was granted even though Pennsylvania governors continued to have authority until the Revolutionary War.

> Maryland was for the Virgin Mary surely named.
> For Roman Catholic settlers, church freedom was obtained,
> But much religious fighting continued through the years.
> The king appointed governors, the colony to steer.

Protestants were not the only people who were denied freedom of worship in England. Catholics also were persecuted. A nobleman named **George Calvert**, whose title was **Lord Baltimore**, served in the court of King Charles. The king granted him a **charter** to establish a land where Catholics could freely practice their faith. Religious freedom was established for others as well. A charter was a document granted to a person giving him possession of a specified piece of land which was owned by the king. The person became the owner of the land and he could sell it or grant it to anyone of his choosing. He could also make the laws in that land. The laws had to be agreed to by the people who lived there and could not be contrary to the laws of England. Though Lord Baltimore died before he could go to America, his son became the first governor of the land which was first named **St. Mary's.**

When the first 200 settlers came, they had friendly relations with the Indians and paid them for the land which they took over. Actually, less than half the settlers were Catholic. The rest were Protestants. Religious freedom was an almost unknown concept in those days. The governor tried to discourage quarrels between the Catholics and Protestants but was not very successful. In 1649, the Legislature of Maryland passed a law called **The Act of Toleration**, which granted freedom of religion. It was the first such law formally passed in the colonies of England. Because of this religious infighting, which continued even after this act was passed, the King eventually was forced to appoint new governors to keep peace in the colony.

> New Jersey was discovered back in 1524.
> One hundred years thereafter, Swedes and Dutchmen came ashore.
> The Englishmen then conquered Dutch possessions in the land.
> Religious freedom reigned when Quaker owners took their stand.

New Jersey was discovered when the famous explorer, **Henry Hudson**, sailed up the river which now bears his name. The land to the east of the river became New York. The land to the west became New Jersey. The first Dutchmen settled in New York. They also believed they had a claim over that land on the other side of the Hudson River, just as they thought they owned Delaware.

In those years when the Dutch came to New York, New Jersey remained unoccupied. So Swedish settlers from Delaware moved in and tried to settle the land. They were evicted by the Dutch in 1660.

The English, the most powerful nation in the New World, did not want the Dutch to take too much of the land. So when they sailed warships into New York Harbor, the Dutch surrendered not only New York, but also New Jersey and Delaware. In return, the Dutch settlers were treated fairly by the British. Their property was not confiscated, and complete religious freedom was granted.

New Jersey was first granted to the **Duke of York**. He then sold it to two of his friends who gave the colony its name. One of the men sold his property to a group of **Quakers** who established the first Quaker colony in America. The Quakers believed in religious freedom for all, and they attracted people of many religious faiths to their land.

The French and the Dutch both occupied New York,
But English armies took control in 1664.
The Dutch and English trappers with the Indians did trade,
But French and English wars, the white men's settlement delayed,

The Dutch were the first people to set up trading posts in the land which would later become the colony of New York. While the English had generally claimed all of North America in 1497, they did not occupy New York. Though Henry Hudson was himself an Englishman, he was working for the Dutch, so he claimed all of the land which he explored for Holland.

During the early 1600's, the French claimed and occupied Canada. Since there was no firmly established boundary in those days, the French felt their claim also included New York. The land was rich in furs, and both the French and the Dutch traded with the Indians in this profitable fur trade.

The Dutch bought Manhattan Island from the Indians for $24. They called it **New Amsterdam** and later, New Netherlands. In 1664, King Charles II decided it was time to claim all the land.

New Amsterdam 1656

England thought all of the land in this part of North America rightfully belonged to them. The King granted a charter to the Duke of York, but there was one provision. The Duke had to conquer the land. When he sailed warships into New York Harbor, the Dutch governor knew he could not defeat the more powerful British.

The Duke promised the Dutch fair treatment and kept his word. The Dutch kept their farms and were not forced out in any way. The name of the land was changed to New York, and the name of the city was changed to New York City.

> *The Puritans and Pilgrims settled Massachusetts' shores.*
> *They sought religious freedom from their British overlords.*
> *They were friendly with the Indians who helped them to survive,*
> *But over foreign politics with the English they did strive.*

The story of the Pilgrims who settled in Plymouth is very well known. The Pilgrims were called **Separatists**. They disagreed with the Church of England and separated from it. Another group of religious dissenters in England was called the **Puritans**. They did not want to leave the church. They only wanted to purify or make it better. They were also persecuted in England. In 1630, three thousand Puritans came to New England and settled just north of the Plymouth Colony. They called their colony the Massachusetts Bay Colony and established the city of Boston.

This was one of the fastest growing areas of the New World. In just ten years, by 1640, there were over 20,000 people in Massachusetts. Many towns were established. Representative government was established in those early days, and each of the towns had their representatives in the colonial government.

During the 1620's, the settlers of Plymouth had very friendly relations with the Indians. This continued as long as Chief Massasoit was alive. However, his son, King Philip, distrusted the white settlers and sought to wipe them out. A war, which was called **King Philip's War,** broke out in 1675. Hundreds of settlers and Indians were killed. It ended in 1676 when King Philip was killed.

King Philip

Massachusetts was one of the first colonies to have problems with the English government. England said that the colonists could trade only with people in England. The Massachusetts colonists wanted to conduct trade with people in other countries as well. These problems continued through the years and became part of the cause of the American Revolution.

Puritan Meeting House

The settlers of Connecticut from Massachusetts came.
Founded small religious colonies in their churches'
names.
They wanted independence from the King of England's laws.
They were among the first to speak their mind in
freedom's cause.

The Puritans who settled Massachusetts had been persecuted in England because of their religious beliefs. The King of England would not tolerate beliefs different than his own. Unfortunately, the Puritans in Massachusetts were not very tolerant of differing beliefs either. For that reason, certain ministers from Massachusetts established towns in Connecticut. The first one, established by **Thomas Hooker** in 1636, was named Hartford.

Connecticut was the first colony to have a document similar to a constitution. The document was called **The Fundamental Orders of Connecticut**. Like their neighbors in Massachusetts, the colonists in Connecticut were in disagreement with the way that England administered the colonies. The thought of freedom from England began very early in the colony of Connecticut.

Those who formed Rhode Island came from Massachusetts, too;
To practice their religion without government ado.
The land was rich and fertile, their ports were hubs of trade.
Independent church and state foundations there were laid.

Rhode Island was also started by people who fled from Massachusetts for religious reasons. The most famous of these was a Puritan minister named **Roger Williams**, who founded a village and called it Providence. At that time, no colony had complete religious freedom. The governments of the colonies were controlled by churches or were actually a part of the churches. Roger Williams believed there should be no connection between the church and the government, and that no person should be forced to be a member of a church, or even to attend church unless they wanted to do so.

He was also the first to establish complete political freedom in a colony. His policies of religious freedom and political freedom attracted many people. Rhode Island became a very prosperous colony because of its fine port and its rich farm land.

New Hampshire was established by decision of King James.
Two English noblemen were given major land domains.
At first, it was a part of Massachusetts colony.
The king, the land divided so they'd function separately.

The Thirteen Colonies

In 1623, a group of woodsmen came to New Hampshire to cut lumber and catch fish, both of which would be sold in England. They did not come to settle the area, but rather to work there temporarily. At first, the settlers of the Massachusetts Bay Colony considered the area to be theirs. It was the King who made it a separate colony when he granted the land to two of his friends.

> *King James gave a charter to a man named, William Penn,*
> *A land once owned by Sweden and the Netherlands.*
> *The Quakers for religious freedom ventured to this land.*
> *They were first to place the government in the people's hands.*

In 1615, a Dutch explorer first sailed up the Delaware River to the place which is now Philadelphia. No one really settled there, however, until about 1643 when people from Sweden established a settlement. **Peter Stuyvesant,** the Dutch governor of New York, captured and ruled the colony until 1664. In that year the Duke of York defeated the Dutch in New York, taking control.

Peter Stuyvescant

After that time, England owned all of the land of the original thirteen colonies. King James owed money to the father of William Penn. His father had been an Admiral in the British Navy and was a very wealthy man. Instead of paying Admiral Penn's son with money, he gave him a land grant in America.

William Penn had become a member of a religious group called the **Quakers**. They did not have religious freedom in England. Neither could they have such freedom in any of the American colonies. Penn welcomed people of all religions and gave them complete religious freedom. He was also the first to put government totally in the hands of the people. Other colonies at that time were ruled by governors appointed by the king. No other colony had placed so much power in the hands of the people.

> *These colonies, at first, behaved like independent states.*
> *But all were ruled by England through the monarch's designates.*
> *Some were loyal to the king, while others soon rebelled.*
> *One day they got together; a new nation they beheld.*

The thirteen colonies were all originally established by Europeans. The British, the Dutch, the Swedes, the French and the Spaniards all had claimed parts of the North American continent. By the year 1664, however, the English were in complete control of the area occupied by the original thirteen colonies..

The French owned most of the land between these colonies and the Mississippi River. The Spaniards owned Florida and the lands of the American West, though very few of them actually lived there.

During the 1700's, events unfolded which gave most of the land controlled by France to the English. The stage was then set for the American Revolutionary War which created a new nation, the United States of America.

Study Questions:

1. Do you think the people who decided to come to America fully understood the dangers they faced? What do you think motivated them to come?

2. When Europeans set foot on American soil, they claimed the land for their kings, yet they knew there were native people already living there? Why do you think they disregarded the Indians as owners of the land?

3. What would have been the proper way to deal with the Indians concerning ownership of the land?

4. The English knew that the French had a claim to the northern part of North America, and the Spaniards had laid claim to the southern parts of the land. Why do you think the English felt they had any right to the land at all?

5. Would it ever be right for people today to go to a foreign land and claim it for themselves? Why or why not?

6. The British people displaced the Dutch, the Swedish, the French and the Spaniards in establishing various colonies in North America for themselves. Do you think they had a right to do this?

7. If a country has superior military power, do they have a right to displace another people over control of a piece of land? Under what conditions might this be okay?

8. The founders of Massachusetts came to the land because of religious persecution. Then, they began to force their religion on all the people in their land. Why do you think they felt they had a right to do this?

9. Is it ever acceptable or proper for a government to force one religious view on all people? Where is this done in the world today? Is it right for people of differing views to rebel against such tyranny?

The Revolutionary War

About the music...
(Tape 1, Song 4)

Using the fife and drum style that is usually associated with the period of the Revolutionary War, this music is done in a traditional march format. If you have ever seen a dramatic re-enactment of that war, you have probably seen the Redcoats in their colorful uniforms marching to this type of music.

The primary instruments you hear are the fife, drums, harpsichord, and the hammered dulcimer. The fife is a flute-like instrument. The hammered dulcimer looks something like a modern day autoharp except the strings are struck by wooden hammers. (The harpsichord, an early keyboard instrument similar to the piano, has strings which are mechanically plucked rather than stricken with felt hammers.) Because of the cheerful mood of victory in the song, it is played in a major key.

In 1763, the British had victory.
    They won the French and Indian War. Their strength was plain to see.
They owned the land of Canada and all the American South.
    From the coast of Nova Scotia to the Mississippi's mouth.

Chorus

Get ready, me boys and call to arms, now what are ye waitin' for?
    The Americans got to win the Revolutionary War.

The English had the colonies under their control;
    There were thirteen separate governments to do as the King extolled.
They reasoned the Americans should pay the English crown,
    For the British troops defended all their villages and towns.

Parliament made the laws that ruled the colonists' fate.
    But colonial representatives could not participate.
They told where they could sail their ships and sell their goods in trade,
    And made them pay stiff taxes on the things that England made.

Chorus

In 1773, the people's remedy
    Was to boycott English products like sugar, coffee and tea.
The merchants back in England began to feel a loss.
    They petitioned to the Parliament to cut the taxes' cost.

Still acting stubbornly, the British taxed the tea.
    Bostonians dumped a cargo load one night into the sea.
The Boston Tea Party brought anger to the King.
    He blockaded Boston Harbor with the goods the ships could bring.

Chorus

In 1774, freedom was the cause.
    The Continental Congress formed to protest British laws.
They told the folks to arm themselves in case of a British attack.
    The colonists would defend themselves and strike the Redcoats back.

In 1775, the battle flag unfurled.
    From Lexington and Concord came "the shot heard round the world."
Paul Revere shouted the warning. The Minutemen came out.
    They drove the Brits to Boston town and showed they had some clout.

Chorus

At the Battle of Bunker Hill, the bloodiest day of the War,
    The British drove the colonists from the hill they were fightin' for.
Then, the colonists formed an army, a rough and tumble band,
    Who fought the Redcoats bravely for the conquest of the land.

The Continental Congress met again in '75;
    Formed the Continental Army to keep the fight alive.
They retook the town of Boston and drove the British out,
    But the war was just beginning and the outcome was in doubt.

Chorus

They fought the war in Canada and in Southern colonies.
    But in '75, the British seemed to have the victory.
Some Americans still were loyal to the British crown.
    They even joined the redcoats, the uprising to put down.

In 1776, the Congress met again;
    Declared their independence from the British ruler, then,
They wrote a Declaration to tell the world just why
    Their right to split from England was most surely justified.

Chorus

It said that from the people came the right of governing;
> That the laws of nature and nature's God were greater than the King.
It listed the abuses of the British crown
> And declared the thirteen colonies were independent now.

Philadelphia was captured one year later by King George.
> Americans spent the winter months in the town of Valley Forge.
They suffered many hardships, and many of them died;
> But noble General Washington, on God he still relied.

Chorus

The colonies needed allies to help with supplies and men.
> They called on England's rivals, the nations of France and Spain.
Vic'try at Saratoga proved the Yanks could win.
> So the allies sent the ships and guns to help the war to end.

In western lands, the British troops with Indians allied;
> To try to force the patriots from the countryside.
In Illinois and Indiana, American troops did reign
> To oust the British army from the claim to western plains.

Chorus

In '78, the southern states entered in the war.
> To Georgia and Carolina marched the British army corps.
In two long years, the patriots in the countryside did fight
> To take the land that England won. They fought with all their might.

In 1781, to Yorktown they did run.
> The French had sent their Navy just to help the Americans.
They surrounded British forces on both the land and sea
> 'til Cornwallis did surrender, and the colonies were free.

Chorus

In 1783, at long last they did sign
> The Treaty of Paris at the Palace of Versailles.
After seven years of fighting, they had their victory.
> The United States of America, a nation now could be.

Chorus

The Revolutionary War

"Is life so dear or peace so sweet as to be purchased at the price of chains and slavery? Forbid it, Almighty God. I know not what course others may take, but as for me, give me liberty or give me death!"
-Patrick Henry, speech to the Virginia Revolutionary Council at St. John's Church, Richmond, VA, 1775.

In 1763, the British had victory.
They won the French and Indian War. Their strength was plain to see.
They owned the land of Canada and all the American South.
From the coast of Nova Scotia to the Mississippi's mouth.

Chorus

Get ready, me boys, and call to arms, now what are ye waitin' for?
The Americans got to win the Revolutionary War.

During the colonial period in America, the French occupied what is now the country of Canada. The principal products were furs. The French were not interested in building farms and occupying the land. They sent unmarried men to live in the land. These trappers developed friendly relations with the Indians since their trade depended on it.

The French also claimed the lands of the Mississippi Valley for France. England believed they also had a claim to this land. When the English colonists began moving to the West in the early 1700s they began to clash with the French. (In those days, when men spoke of the West, they referred to places like western Pennsylvania, Ohio, Indiana and Illinois. Today we call that area the Midwest.) The colonists were interested in clearing the land and establishing farms and communities, while the French were interested in maintaining the wilderness in its native state. Otherwise, their trade in furs and skins would be decreased as the land was claimed by farms.

Naturally, the Indians in the region sided with the French. Trappers were far better acquainted with the Indians than were the English. Because trappers traded with the Indians on a regular basis, they were more familiar with their languages. Some trappers even lived with the Indians. They convinced them that the English would take away the land and destroy their hunting grounds. There was truth in these words. So a great conflict between the English and the French was under way in the 1700's.

In Europe, the French and English were not friends either. They had many disputes, one of their biggest being the control of the New World. Both nations laid claim to the vast unoccupied lands.

But who would take possession and occupy the land?

The French built forts in the Ohio territory and in Pennsylvania to strengthen their claim. They also built forts on the Mississippi River all the way down to New Orleans. Finally, the colonists in Virginia, whose claim to the same land went back to the settlement of Jamestown in 1609, decided to do something about this situation. The British governor sent a trustworthy young man named **George Washington** to deliver a message to the French general in command of the Ohio country, telling him to leave the territory because it belonged to the British. The French general politely replied that the land belonged to France.

Between 1754 and 1763, the English fought many battles with the French who had formed an alliance with most of the Indians in the territory. After nine years of skirmishes, the English finally won. These battles were a part of what came to be called **The French and Indian War**. The principal French settlement in the New World was Quebec. If the English could capture that city, they would be in control of the North American continent. In 1763, an army of 5,000 British soldiers were successful in capturing Quebec. **The Treaty of Paris** signed in 1763 gave all of the land east of the Mississippi to England and the land west of the Mississippi to Spain. In return, Spain gave Florida to England.

Finally, England established its control over North America. English colonists then began to occupy more and more of the lands in the states now known as Ohio, Indiana, Illinois and Missouri.

> *The English had the colonies under their control;*
> *There were thirteen separate governments to do as the King extolled.*
> *They reasoned the Americans should pay the English crown,*
> *For the British troops defended all their villages and towns.*

Indeed, the British had sent troops to defend the colonists and to win the French and Indian War. To fight such a war was very costly. Also, there were many British troops still stationed in the colonies, and they had to be paid. The King thought the colonists should pay a large part of that cost.

Minuteman Statue

> *Parliament made the laws that ruled the colonists' fate.*
> *But colonial representatives could not participate.*
> *They told where they could sail their ships and sell their goods in trade,*
> *And made them pay stiff taxes on the things that England made.*

The businesses in the colonies could not conduct trade with other countries on their own. They could not send ships to other countries.

They could trade only with England. Also, the English Parliament decided to raise money by levying special taxes on the colonists. All of the merchandise purchased in the colonies was either made in England or shipped from England.

Stamp Act

One such law raising taxes was called the **Stamp Act**. Colonists had to purchase stamps which had to be placed on any documents made on paper. This included everything from newspapers to books to marriage certificates and other official government documents. The colonists thought this was unfair since they had no representatives in Parliament. They thought the King was breaking his own laws which granted all Englishmen representation in Parliament.

> *In 1773, the people's remedy*
> *Was to boycott English products like sugar, coffee and tea.*
> *The merchants back in England began to feel a loss.*
> *They petitioned to the Parliament to cut the taxes' cost.*

The colonists fought back in their own way. When they refused to buy products made in England, the British merchants began to suffer. Their sales were much lower, and they lost money. This is called a **boycott**. Then, the merchants petitioned their representatives in Parliament to cut the extra taxes on the colonists so their sales would increase as before.

The colonists and the English began to have other problems. English troops were sent to keep the peace and to help enforce the laws. In an incident known as the **Boston Massacre**, five colonists were killed in a skirmish between colonists and soldiers. This incident was highly publicized, and news of it spread throughout the colonies, causing much ill feeling toward the British.

Finally, the British felt the colonists' pressure and cut the taxes on products. However, they continued to tax one product, tea, just to show that they still had the right to levy taxes.

> *Still acting stubbornly, the British taxed the tea.*
> *Bostonians dumped a cargo load one night into the sea.*
> *The Boston Tea Party brought anger to the King.*
> *He blockaded Boston Harbor with the goods the ships could bring.*

The **Boston Tea Party** is one of the most famous events of American History. It occurred three years after the Boston Massacre. During these years, the people still refused to buy tea from England. **King George III** decided to act with strength and decisiveness. He sent three ships to Boston with full cargo of tea. He was going to force them to buy tea from England. A group of colonists disguised themselves as Indians, boarded the ships, and dumped the tea overboard. The King could not afford to suffer disgrace. He felt he had to respond to this outrageous deed.

He, therefore, sent the British Navy to Boston to **blockade** the port until the people of the city paid for all of the tea. This meant the Navy would not allow any trading ships to enter the harbor. Without trading ships, the people of Boston and New England could not receive food and all the other products they needed for their daily lives. The people in the other colonies responded by sending food overland to the people of New England.

> *In 1774, freedom was the cause.*
> *The Continental Congress formed to protest British laws.*
> *They told the folks to arm themselves in case of a British attack.*
> *The colonists would defend themselves and strike the Redcoats back.*

The people of all the colonies realized the problem with their mother country was becoming more severe. It was time for them to meet together and unite. Therefore, they sent delegates to a meeting known as the **Continental Congress**. Rather than issue protests by themselves, the colonies spoke with a united voice and asked Parliament to give them their proper rights as Englishmen. It was not their purpose to seek independence at that time. Only a few men were preaching this message of independence. The Congress simply wanted to appeal to the king and the Parliament for their rights.

The king reacted with a show of force. He sent British army units to Massachusetts. He thought this would frighten the people and force them to obey his laws. Instead, the people began to arm themselves. They formed militias of colonists. A **militia** is a military unit consisting of local volunteer soldiers. One such group in Massachusetts was called the "**Minutemen**." They gave themselves this name because they said they could be ready to fight at a minute's notice.

> *In 1775, the battle flag unfurled.*
> *From Lexington and Concord came "the shot heard round the world."*
> *Paul Revere shouted the warning. The Minutemen came out.*
> *They drove the Brits to Boston town and showed they had some clout.*

The people who opposed English rule and wanted freedom from England were called **patriots**. Those who supported the king, even though they disagreed with some of his actions, were called **Loyalists** or **Tories**. British soldiers were called "**redcoats**" because of the bright red coats that were part of their uniforms. The British heard the colonists were storing weapons and ammunition in two towns near Boston— Lexington and Concord. They sent an army of redcoats to those towns to capture the weapons and to arrest leaders of this army of patriots.

Paul Revere

Another very famous person in American History is **Paul Revere**, a silversmith, who was a devoted patriot. He was the man who heard of the British plan to attack Lexington and Concord. He rode ahead of the army and warned the Minutemen of the attack.

The militia of patriots assembled and faced the British. As they stood facing each other on April 18, 1775, someone fired a shot. No one knows for sure who fired that first shot or which side he was on. But that shot started the **Battles of Lexington and Concord**, which were the first battles of the **American Revolution**. That famous shot became known as "the shot heard 'round the world." At this point, no one had declared war, but a war had begun nonetheless.

> At the Battle of Bunker Hill, the bloodiest day of the War,
> The British drove the colonists from the hill they were fightin' for.
> Then, the colonists formed an army, a rough and tumble band,
> Who fought the Redcoats bravely for the conquest of the land.

The people in Boston had formed a large militia of over 1,000 men. Two months after the **Battle of Lexington**, they planned another attack to try to force the powerful British Army out of Boston. The colonists' militia ran out of ammunition and lost that battle, but showed that they were a brave military force that would not easily quit.

> The Continental Congress met again in '75;
> Formed the Continental Army to keep the fight alive.
> They retook the town of Boston and drove the British out,
> But the war was just beginnin' though the outcome was in doubt.

Actually, the **Second Continental Congress** began meeting even before the **Battle of Bunker Hill**. Still, most of the representatives did not want to sever their ties with England at that time. They simply wanted King George to change his mind and treat them justly, allowing them to have the same freedoms as Englishmen in England. This Congress met for over a year. They decided to form the **Continental Army** and place **George Washington** in charge of that army.

During the time the Congress was meeting, King George did not change his mind. In fact, he did just the opposite. He decided to use even more force to keep the American colonists in line. Since it was hard to raise an army of Englishmen to fight against the Americans, he hired German soldiers called **Hessians** to fight for him. Now, most colonists who had previously been loyal to the King became Patriots.

> They fought the war in Canada and in Southern colonies.
> But in '75, the British seemed to have the victory.
> Some Americans still were loyal to the British crown.
> They even joined the redcoats, the uprising to put down.

Prior to 1775, the desire to separate from English was strongest in the northern colonies. In spite of the King's refusal to back down from his oppression of the colonies, still many people were loyal to the king, particularly in the southern colonies. It was there that some people even joined with the British army to help put down the revolution.

Probably the most important act of the Second Continental Congress was their request that a **Declaration of Independence** be written.

The task of writing the Declaration of Independence was given to five members of the Congress including Benjamin Franklin, John Adams and Thomas Jefferson, who actually penned the document.

> In 1776, the Congress met again;
>> Declared their independence from the British ruler, then,
> They wrote a Declaration to tell the world just why
>> Their right to split from England was most surely justified.
>
> It said that from the people came the right of governing;
>> That the laws of nature and nature's God were greater than
>> the king.
> It listed the abuses of the British crown
>> And declared the thirteen colonies were independent now.

The Declaration said that all men are created equal, and they deserve basic rights such as life, liberty, and the pursuit of happiness not because of the gracious desire of the king, but because God, the Creator, gave them these rights. It also declared that the right to rule or govern comes from the people who are being governed and that when a ruler violates his responsibilities to govern in a just manner, the people have the right to make changes in the government or even abolish that government. They listed all the ways that King George abused his powers and then declared that the colonies were no longer a part of England but were independent states.

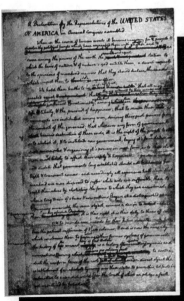

Declaration of Independence

When the members of the Continental Congress signed the declaration, they were placing themselves in very great danger. If England should be able to put down the Revolution and win the war for independence, these men could be arrested, tried for treason, and executed. The Declaration of Independence was signed on **July 4, 1776**. That is why we celebrate that day as **Independence Day**.

New York was a very important colony in the war. England was able to capture its port city early in the war. Since New York City had such a fine, large harbor, it would be easy for the English to send many ships there filled with soldiers and supplies. Also, the colony of New York separated the northern colonies, where most of the unrest and strife had taken place, from the southern colonies who were more loyal to the King.

It appeared that the British army was going to win the war quickly by the end of 1776. But Washington's army won a very important battle, the **Battle of Trenton**, in the state of New Jersey which is just to the west of New York City. The Americans had been very discouraged, but this victory gave them great hope and helped General Washington rebuild the Continental Army so that it could fight again.

> *Philadelphia was captured one year later by King George.*
> *Americans spent the winter months in the town of Valley Forge.*
> *They suffered many hardships, and many of them died;*
> *But noble General Washington, on God he still relied.*

At that point in time, Philadelphia was the principal city of the colonies. It was where the Continental Congress had met, where independence had been declared. The English won a key victory when they were able capture the city. The Continental Congress had to flee to the town of York, Pennsylvania, to run the affairs of the colonies.

Washington and his army of 10,000 men had to retreat. They spent the winter in the town of **Valley Forge**. They had very little food and were very poorly supplied. About 2,500 men died of starvation and exposure. Nonetheless, in the spring, the army began to train for battle once again.

> *The colonies needed allies to help with supplies and men.*
> *They called on England's rivals, the nations of France and Spain.*
> *Vic'try at Saratoga proved the Yanks could win.*
> *So the allies sent the ships and guns to help the war to end.*

Another key battle in the war was fought in upstate New York near the Hudson River where the Patriot armies surrounded the British Army and captured 6,000 prisoners and all their weapons and supplies. That was called the **Battle of Saratoga**. It was the turning point of the war because it proved the Americans were strong enough to win major battles against the British.

Valley Forge

In order to win the war, the Americans needed

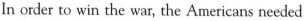

guns, ammunition and ships. They had no factories to make these things themselves, so they had to obtain them from other countries. France and Spain had long been bitter enemies of the English. So it was obvious that the Continental Congress would go to them for help. But France and Spain were not willing to join a losing cause and throw away their money and prestige. First, they wanted to see if the Americans were strong enough to win. The victory at the Battle of Saratoga showed France and Spain all they needed to see. They entered the war on the side of the Americans.

The presence of France and Spain caused many problems for England. The American colonies were not the only lands owned by England in the New World. England also owned many islands in the Atlantic Ocean, places such as Bermuda, Barbados, the Virgin Islands, etc. The king had to send armies to protect these islands because he feared that France and Spain would try to capture them. So he ordered many of his troops in New York and Pennsylvania to sail to the Caribbean Sea to protect those British territories. As the British army moved to New York, they fought with the Americans, but neither side really won. It ended in a draw.

> *In the western lands, the British troops with Indians allied;*
> *To try to force the patriots from the countryside.*
> *In Illinois and Indiana, American troops did reign*
> *To oust the British army from the claim to western plains.*

Just as the French had told the Indians that the English would take away their lands during the French and Indian War, now the English used the same tactic in the Revolutionary War. They told the Indians that if the Americans won the war, they would take away their land. Some of the Indians did side with the British, though many other Indians fought with the Americans. The American army was successful in capturing the forts in the west and won that part of the war.

> *In '78, the southern states entered in the war.*
> *To Georgia and Carolina marched the British army corps.*
> *In two long years, the patriots in the country   side did fight*
> *To take the land that England won. They fought with all their might.*

Since the British could not claim victory in the North, they changed their strategy and decided to fight in the southern colonies where they thought more of the Americans would be loyal to England. They were successful at first. In 1778, the English captured the colonies of South Carolina and Georgia. After several battles in the next two years, the patriots finally recaptured those colonies.

> *In 1781, to Yorktown they did run.*
> *The French had sent their Navy just to help the Americans.*
> *They surrounded British forces on both the land and sea*
> *'til Cornwallis did surrender, and the colonies were free.*

The British moved their army to Yorktown, Virginia, a seaport town. They had planned to send their Navy in to pick up the troops and move them to New York. But with the help of the French navy and the French army, General Washington was able to surround the British on the land and prevent the British ships from rescuing them from the sea. General Cornwallis, the British commander, had to surrender his 8,000 troops. It was a crushing defeat for the British.

> *In 1783, at long last they did sign*
> *The Treaty of Paris at the Palace of Versailles.*
> *After seven years of fighting, they had their victory.*
> *The United States of America, a nation now could be.*

Yorktown was the last major battle of the Revolutionary War, though there were a few minor skirmishes over the next two year. Shortly after Yorktown, the British began to hold peace negotiations with the Americans. The peace talks were held in Paris, France. By November of 1782, the two sides had agreed on terms of peace. The **Treaty of Paris** was ratified by the American Congress on September 3, 1783.

Study Questions:

1. The English government offered many services to the American colonists. Their armies offered protection from aggression by Indians and aggression from other countries. They had provided much of the money for the founding of the colonies. Do you think the king of England had a right to tax and govern the Americans in any way he thought appropriate?

2. Do you think the colonies had the right to be represented in Parliament? Do American territories such as Puerto Rico, Guam, the Pacific Trust Territories, etc, have a right to representation in Congress? Why or why not?

3. Under what conditions do any people have the right to rebel against their government? What actions should a people take before declaring independence?

4. Do you believe the American Colonies did the right thing in declaring independence? Do you think they were justified in doing so?

5. Many citizens in the colonies were opposed to the movement for independence and wanted to remain citizens of England. Do you think they were wrong? Were their rights violated when the patriots prevailed?

6. Would it ever be proper for Americans today to overthrow their government? Under what conditions would this be acceptable?

7. Why do you think the French sided with the Americans during the Revolutionary War?

8. Suppose the Americans had lost the Revolutionary War. What would the English historians have said about men like George Washington and the other founding fathers? If we were British citizens today as a result of such a loss, what would you think of these men? Would you consider them to be brave patriots fighting for what they believed, or would you think of them as traitors?

9. Men can be cast as heroes or villains depending on the outcome of wars, elections, legislative decisions or court verdicts. (The people who win usually become the heroes while the losers are billed as villains.) How, then , can we know the truth about history? How can we believe the things we read in history books?

Signers
of The
Declaration
of
Independence

THE CONSTITUTION

About the music...
(Tape 1, Song 5)

This is done in a style of classical music called a "gavotte." It is also called chamber music. Often we think of people like Bach, Handel, Mozart and Haydn as having lived a thousand years ago. Actually, these famous musicians lived at the same time as George Washington, Benjamin Franklin, Thomas Jefferson and the other founders of our country. The music they wrote was popular and in style during this part of our history.

Have you ever seen formal pictures of George and Martha Washington? In these pictures, they are dressed in the kind of clothing worn at formal balls where this type of music was played. The primary instrument is the harpsichord, the forerunner of the piano. The piano, as we know it, was actually invented around 1850. You also hear bowed stringed instruments such as violins, cellos and the double bass. This type of orchestra is called a chamber orchestra.

In 17 and 81, the thirteen colonies had won
    The Revolutionary War we'd fought with England.
There were thirteen sep'rate states reluctant to cooperate
    And form a union in this new land.

Chorus

The founding fathers' lasting contribution
    Was the Constitution of the United States

The very year the war was o'er, they signed new governing accords,
    The Articles of Confederation.
They guaranteed autonomy and independent sovereignty
    To each dominion in this new land.

Chorus

But this new government was weak, outlook for compromise was bleak.
    They had no authority to levy taxes.
All thirteen states had to agree to then accomplish anything
    They did together in this new land.

Chorus

In Philadelphia was held a meeting quite unparalleled
    Which they called the Constitutional Convention.
They wrote a document so strong, it would establish right and wrong
    For that great nation in this new land.

Chorus

A new republic was conceived. No man could ever then receive
    Full power over this entire nation.
The people had the right to rule, responsibility to choose
    The ones to govern in this new land.

Chorus

They had a President because he must enforce established laws
    Passed by the Congress of these United States,
An independent Supreme Court to settle problems of all sorts
    Among the people in this new land.

Chorus

To pass the laws, they did create a Congress to facilitate
    The rightful needs and wishes of the people,
Two legislative bodies for Congressmen and Senators
    To pass the statutes in this new land.

Chorus

And for our freedoms to preserve, a Bill of Rights designed to serve
    To guarantee the freedoms of the people.
No government could take away our right to speak and meet and pray,
    Or guard our families in this new land.

Chorus

This nation ne'er would have a king; a monarchy could only bring
    Excesses caused by independent power.
A president they would elect with a sworn duty to protect
    The Constitution of this new land.

Chorus

The Constitution

"We may be tossed upon an ocean where we can see no land—nor, perhaps, the sun or stars. But there is a chart and a compass for us to study, to consult, and to obey. That chart is the Constitution."

-Daniel Webster

In 17 and 81, the thirteen colonies had won
   The Revolutionary War we'd fought with England.
There were thirteen sep'rate states reluctant to cooperate
   And form a union in this new land.

The last major battle of the Revolutionary War had been fought in October of 1781. The war was not immediately over at that point, however. There were a few minor skirmishes in the next year or so. Also, British troops were still stationed in America.

Peace negotiations began shortly after the Battle of Yorktown in Paris, France. About two years later, England and the new United States signed a treaty called the **Treaty of Paris**. A **treaty** is a peace agreement signed between countries. In this treaty, England agreed that the United States was an independent nation, and the borders were established. The nation was bounded by Canada on the North, the Atlantic on the East, the Mississippi River on the West, and Florida on the South.

At the end of the French and Indian War in 1763, Florida had become the possession of England as the result of the Treaty of Paris. During the Revolutionary War, the Spaniards regained control of Florida from the British, whose forces were busy fighting in other areas. Spain owned most of the lands in the Western States. Their land included what is now Texas, Arizona, New Mexico, Utah, and most of what is now Colorado and California. The land to the northwest of the Spanish territory was called the Northwest Territory.

The colonies were now a nation; however, they functioned like thirteen independent countries. They were distrustful of a big central government, especially one that was far away from their state.

The very year the war was o'er, they signed new governing accords,
   The Articles of Confederation.
They guaranteed autonomy and independent sovereignty
   To each dominion in this new land.

Discussion of **The Articles of Confederation** actually began during the Revolutionary War. The Second Continental Congress, the same one that declared independence from England, actually wrote a draft of the Articles even before independence was declared on July 4, 1776. A **draft** is a document that is written before it is agreed upon. All the representatives could then read the draft and make suggestions for changes before they would vote to agree upon it. The Congress debated the language in the draft for years. It was not adopted or agreed upon until March, 1781.

The name of the nation, **The United States of America**, came from The Articles of Confederation. The central government had power to raise up an army and a navy, issue currency, borrow money, control Indian affairs, and declare war and peace. All other functions of government were controlled by the individual states.

The Articles declared the sovereignty and autonomy of the states. **Sovereignty** means that each state has independent power and authority and that no state has greater power than any other state. **Autonomy** means that no other state could tell it how to conduct its affairs.

> *But this new government was weak, outlook for compromise was bleak;*
> *They had no authority to levy taxes.*
> *All thirteen states had to agree to then accomplish anything*
> *They did together in this new land.*

The **Congress** consisted of one representative from each state, no matter how large it was or how many people it had. Each representative had one vote. Most importantly, the Congress could not levy taxes. Funds had to be donated by the states. Without the power to collect tax money, the government had very little power. The new leaders tried to amend the Articles, but in order for an amendment to be passed, all thirteen states had to agree. It was almost impossible, therefore, for the Congress to accomplish anything.

> *In Philadelphia was held a meeting quite unparalleled*
> *Which they called the Constitutional Convention.*
> *They wrote a document so strong, it would establish right   And wrong for that great*
> *nation in this new land.*

In 1787, the states agreed to hold a **Constitutional Convention** to revise The Articles of Confederation. Instead of revising them, however, the Convention chose to abandon them and frame a new **Constitution**. In writing a new constitution, the delegates knew the difficulty they faced in creating a government. They had seen and experienced oppressive governments like the ones in Europe, and they greatly valued the freedom they experienced in their own states. They knew they needed to strike a very delicate balance.

Ben Franklin

Each state wanted to have a certain amount of independence because people in different parts of the country have different beliefs, culture, and economic needs. A southern state with an agricultural economy would have different needs than a northern state with an industrial economy. A predominately Catholic state might wish to have different laws than a predominately Protestant state. But the central government needed to be strong enough to keep the states united so they would have the power of a large nation. For example, if a foreign power were to attack any part of the nation, all of the states would need to act in a unified manner and join in the defense of the country. Another problem was the lack of a unified currency. Prior to 1792, each state produced its own kind of money. This made travel and commerce between the states very difficult. The central government would provide one kind of money that could be used in every state rather than having each state coin its own kind of money.

> *A new republic was conceived no man could ever then receive*
>   *Full power over this entire nation.*
> *The people had the right to rule, responsibility to choose*
>   *The ones to govern in this new land.*

In designing a new government for this country, the delegates to the Constitutional Convention had to decide what kind of government they wanted. They certainly did not want a **monarchy** that had a king in control like they had in England. A king could rule with injustice and take away the freedom of the people.

Another type of government they could have chosen was a pure **democracy** where all of the power would have been placed in the hands of the people. They knew that if the people had the right to vote on every matter, they could act as wrongly as an evil king.

The type of government they chose was called a **republic**. This is a type of government that does not have a king, but has an elected chief, usually called a **President**. It places the ultimate power in the hands of the people who elect their rulers. The object of the republic they created was to make sure that no one person or group had all the power in its hand.

> *They had a President because he must enforce established laws*
>   *Passed by the Congress of these United States,*
> *An independent Supreme Court to settle problems of all sorts*
>   *Among the people in this new land.*

The Constitution defined the powers of the elected President. The President would not have full power over all the laws like a king. He was charged with very specific responsibilities. It would be his job to enforce the laws which were passed by the legislative, or law-making, branch of government. The President would have the power to appoint other people who would preside over agencies of many people who would enforce the many different kinds of laws.

Also, the President would not have power to act as a judge in court cases. The Constitution established a branch of government called the **Judicial Branch** to do this. The President could recommend or nominate people to be judges, but the Congress had to **confirm** or agree with the President before these people could become judges.

> *To pass the laws, they did create a Congress to facilitate*
>   *The rightful needs and wishes of the people,*
> *Two legislative bodies for Congressmen and Senators*

To pass the statutes in this new land.

The Constitution also told the way that laws would be made. **Laws** are rules that all people in the nation must obey. Again, the President would not have the power to make laws. This was to be done by a group of people who also had to be elected by the people. This group is called the **Congress**. The people of each state would elect two kinds of representatives in Congress. Every state, regardless of size or population, would have two **Senators**. The people of each state would also elect members of the **House of Representatives**. The more people there were in a state, the more representatives they would have. These men are called Representatives or Congressmen. They are most often referred to as **Congressmen**.

The decision to have two houses of Congress was a **compromise**. A compromise is an agreement made by two or more groups of people with different opinions on a subject. A compromise is a solution to the disagreement with which all groups can be satisfied. The smaller states thought it would be unfair for the larger states to have more representatives, since all states were supposed to be equal. The larger states thought it would be unfair for smaller states with fewer people to have just as much power as the more populous states. The compromise created two houses of Congress, both of which would have to agree upon the laws which would be passed.

> *And for our freedoms to preserve, a Bill of Rights designed to serve*
> *To guarantee the freedoms of the people.*
> *No government could take away our right to speak and meet and pray,*
> *Or guard our families in this new land.*

The delegates to the Constitutional Convention knew that people could easily lose their rights and freedoms if the Congress were to pass certain types of laws. Therefore, immediately after the Constitution was **ratified**, or agreed upon, by the people, they added a new section to it called an **amendment**. The first ten amendments to the Constitution are called the **Bill of Rights**. It stated that Congress could never pass laws which would remove or take away certain basic rights and freedoms that all people have.

These include such rights as freedom of speech, freedom of the press, freedom of assembly, freedom of religion, the right to keep and bear arms, and the right for a person accused of a crime to have a trial by a jury of citizens rather than by a government official.

> *This nation ne'er would have a king; a monarchy could only bring*
> *Excesses caused by independent power.*
> *A president they would elect with a sworn duty to protect*
> *The Constitution of this new land.*

The writers of the Constitution also knew that if a person was given too much power, he might become conceited and corrupt. Therefore, the Constitution provided that elected officials could serve for specific periods of time only and that they had only certain powers. Also, the elected officials had to obey the laws just like everyone else. If they violated a law, they would be punished just like anyone else.

When the nation elects a president, he must take an oath of office promising to protect and defend the Constitution. That means he cannot do whatever he wants. He can only do those things permitted by the Constitution. All other office holders take a similar oath to follow the Constitution. That is why our government is ruled by laws rather than by rulers who have unlimited power to do whatever they want.

Our **Constitutional Republic** was something very unique in the world of that day. In fact, it was the only nation in the world that had a republican form of government with the people electing their leaders. In coming years, other nations would follow the example set by the founding fathers of our country.

Thomas Jefferson

Study Questions:

1. Study the meaning of the words "autonomy" and "sovereignty" from this and other sources and explain in your own words the meaning of the terms. Give examples which illustrate the meaning of these terms.

2. Suppose the colonies had continued as sovereign and autonomous states rather than uniting under a Constitution. What would have happened to the Union? Would the colonies have united and worked together as one country? Would they have gone their own separate ways? What other scenarios could have resulted? What do you think?

3. What do you think is the difference between having a loose confederation of states and a strong national or federal government? Which do you think would be better? Why?

4. Under The Articles of Confederation, the states were like separate little countries with a loose agreement binding them together. What might have been the advantage in being only loosely united together?

5. What advantages and disadvantages did the colonies have in adopting a constitution which would define the rights and powers of the Federal Government of the United States?

6. What are the differences between a monarchy, a democracy and a republic?

7. Show examples of each of these kinds of governments in the world today.

8. Which type of government do you think would be the best? Tell why you think this is true.

9. What do you think it means that the President enforces established laws? How does he do this?

10. What is the difference between making laws and enforcing the laws?

11. The Congress of the United States is made up of two houses, the Senate and the House of Representatives. What are the advantages of having two houses of Congress? What are the disadvantages?

12. Why can't the President just make up his own rules according to what he thinks is right and make everyone obey and submit to those rules?

13. What is the most important factor in establishing the rule of law in the United States—the Constitution or the will of the majority of the people?

14. In the President's oath of office which he takes on the day of his inauguration, he swears that he will, to the best of his ability, "preserve, protect, and defend the Constitution of the United States." Why don't they just ask him to swear that he will rule the people to the best of his ability? What's the difference between these things?

15. If the President thought it was not right for you to start a magazine which criticized the President, why couldn't he simply order you not to do it?

Signing of Constitution, Presided by George Washington

The Civil War

About the music...
(Tape 2, Song 1)

This ballad is done in a typical folk music style that would have been heard during the Civil War. The instruments you hear are the guitar, the flute, and the harmonica. These were the types of instruments soldiers would have used during the war to entertain themselves. Though you often hear about the famous battles, you must remember that most of a soldier's life was spent in camps and in rather dull activities. Music was a way of escape from the drudgery of the war.

The music is in a minor key to portray the sadness of the Civil War. A tragic event such as this really could not be musically depicted in any other way.

The Civil War started in 1861.
    The North and the South faced each other with a gun.
They fought for four long years through snow and summer's heat.
    In 1865, the South faced its defeat.

Chorus

And the War raged on
    Furious as could be;
Six-hundred thousand soldiers died,
    A tragic victory.

The Union states were in the North,
    Confederates in the South.
One issue then was slavery;
    Of that there was no doubt.
The South said that slavery had always been their way.
    The North said, "No, no man should be another person's slave."

Still others said the issue was a state's authority;
    To say what should be right or wrong within their boundaries.
Could the nation force its will against a state's own sovereignty?
    Or could a state secede and break the nation's unity?

Chorus

Abe Lincoln was the President of the Union states.
  Jeff Davis led the South in those years of strife and hate.
Ulysees S. Grant was Northern General in Chief.
  Confederate Commander was Robert E. Lee.

In South Carolina, down in Charleston bay, Ft. Sumter fell to Southern troops,
  The war was under way.
The Southern boys took over that island fortress then,
  And held it till the war was almost at its end.

Chorus

In Virginia at Manassas, the first Battle of Bull Run,
  The South and North collided, but the Southern army won.
It gave the South much confidence. They thought that they could win.
  It made the War much longer than it would have ever been.

The North had lots of factories for guns and ships and shells.
  The South relied on money crops, tobacco, cotton bales.
The Confederates sent to Europe for the armaments of war,
  But when the Union blocked their ports, the South received no more.

Chorus

Not only was it fought on land, but also on the sea.
  The South owned the Merrimac; it fought ingeniously.
It clashed with the Monitor, that frigate of the North.
  Those ironclad vessels changed the course of Naval war.

In '62, the Union charged the capital of the South
  To cut the railroad lines and knock their major armies out.
Confederate Army soldiers held their capital that day;
  But lost some major battles in old Virgin-i-a.

Chorus

The Shenandoah Valley was the path through which they surged
  To a town in Pennsylvania by the name of Gettysburg.
Lee's troops were devastated, were forced into retreat.
  It turned the tide against the South in July of '63.

On the Mississippi River, the Union troops attacked
  To stop the Southern armies and split the South in half.
They captured ol' New Orleans and finally Vicksburg,
  And after that, the South was practically deterred.

Chorus

Bull Run and Antietam, Cold Harbor, Fredericksburg,
  Perryville and Nashville, Stone Harbor, and Vicksburg,
Chattanooga, Chickamauga, Shiloh, Mobile Bay
  Were the names of famous battles in our nation's darkest day.

In the final year of war, Grant fought furiously;
  He captured Virginia and finally Tennessee.
In the state of Alabama, he captured Mobile Bay,
  And when he routed Nashville, the end was on its way.

Chorus

In the Battle of Atlanta, Gen'ral Sherman with his might,
  Destroyed that Southern city, ravaged everything in sight.
He marched on to Savannah, burning cities, fields, and inns.
  That's why they say that Georgia, then, was gone with the wind.

When Grant captured Richmond in 1865,
  The Southern troops were finished; Lee could not survive.
At a place called Appomattox in Virginia, one day,
  The Confederacy surrendered, and the South was held at bay.
Chorus

The Civil War

"I am sick and tired of war. Its glory is all moonshine. It is only those who have never fired a shot nor heard the shrieks and groans of the wounded who cry aloud for blood, more vengeance, more desolation. War is hell."
- General William T. Sherman, Union General

The Civil War started in 1861.
   The North and the South faced each other with a gun.
They fought for four long years through snow and summer's heat.
   In 1865, the South faced its defeat.

Chorus

And the War raged on
   Furious as could be;
Six-hundred thousand soldiers died,
   A tragic victory.

Of all the periods of American history, the saddest and most tragic of all was the **Civil War**. It was a time when Americans divided and fought against each other. It lasted from 1861 to 1865. The effects of the war have never totally gone away, even to this day.

The Union states were in the North,
   Confederates in the South.
One issue then was slavery;
   Of that there was no doubt.
The South said that slavery had always been their way.
   The North said, "No, no man should be another person's slave."

Still others said the issue was a state's authority;
   To say what should be right or wrong within their boundaries.
Could the nation force its will against a state's own sovereignty?
   Or could a state secede and break the nation's unity?

Why did the Civil War occur? What caused the Southern states to decide to **secede** or separate from the United States and form their own country?

One major issue that divided America in those days was the issue of slavery. Slavery had always been present in America from the very beginning. In 1619, the first shipload of slaves was brought to the colony at Jamestown. For over 200 years, Americans dealt in the slave trade both in the North and in the South. Even the founding fathers of this nation owned slaves.

A few years after the Revolutionary War, a strong movement began in Europe to put an end to the slave trade. By 1807, slavery was illegal in the British Empire.

Slavery began to disappear in the North shortly after 1800. Farms in the North were small, and the owners could not afford slaves anyway. Also, factories began to develop in the North, and people in the cities began working in the factories. Slavery was not necessary or practical in the North. Unfortunately, the predominant reasons for opposition to slavery in the North were economic rather than humanitarian.

The South was very different. The land was very well suited for growing crops like tobacco and cotton. These were called "**money crops,**" as they are today. The world greatly desired these products. But many workers were needed to plant and harvest these crops on the large plantations of the South. Slavery was the answer for the cheap production of these crops which brought enormous wealth to the South from all over the world. Since there were very few factories in the South, agriculture was the means of producing a living for most people. Unfortunately, the economy of the South ran on slave labor.

The North wanted slavery abolished throughout the country. But half the states were "slave" states and half were "free" states.

Most people today consider slavery to be the cause of the Civil War. Other people say that the real issue was whether states had the right to make their own decisions. The South wanted the states to be more independent while the North wanted a more powerful federal government with more decisions to be made by the Congress.

While it is true that the state's rights issue and other issues were important, it would not have been of that much concern had there not been an emotional, moral and economic issue such as slavery. The federal government was trying to force the southern states to totally change their whole way of life.

Another example of an issue which divided the states was **tariffs.** Tariffs are taxes on goods imported from other countries. For example if you had lived in the North and owned a factory which manufactured cotton harvesting machines, you would not want competition from an English company which might be able to

Abraham Lincoln

produce these machines at a lower cost and sell them in the Southern States for a cheaper price. Therefore, you would have been in favor of a law which would require Southern planters to pay big taxes if they bought machines outside the United States. On the other hand, if you had been a farmer in the South, you would have wanted a policy called **free trade** which would have allowed you to buy machines from any company in the world which charged the lowest prices. The issue of tariffs and free trade was a big issue in the mid-nineteenth century and it is a big issue in the United States today, also.

In those days, most of the factories were in the North, so they favored tariffs on manufactured goods. The people in the South had an agricultural economy. Therefore, they were opposed to these taxes. This issue was very complicated. There were other cases where some southerners wanted tariffs. For example, a product called hemp which is used to make rope was produced in the South. Some southerners wanted a tariff to be charged on hemp imported from Russia to protect the Southern hemp producers from foreign competition.

Robert E. Lee

> *Abe Lincoln was the President of the Union states.*
> *Jeff Davis led the South in those years of strife and hate.*
> *Ulysees S. Grant was Northern General in Chief.*
> *Confederate Commander was Robert E. Lee.*

In 1861, South Carolina was the first state to **secede** from, or leave, the Union. They were quickly followed by the other southern states. They formed a new government and called their new nation the **Confederate States of America**. They elected a man named **Jefferson Davis** as their first president.

President Lincoln called for volunteers for an army as soon as the first states left the Union. He was determined to save the Union and keep it together even if it meant war.

Actually, the Union had many generals who served as Commander-in-Chief of its army. The last one to do so was named **Ulysees S. Grant**. He was not that prominent in the earlier days of the war, but his victories in some important battles brought his name to the attention of President Lincoln so that by the end of the war, he was in command. Also, he was later to be elected President.

The Confederacy also had more than one Commander-in-Chief. But the one who served throughout most of the war was the famous **General Robert E. Lee**. Actually, General Lee might have become the commander of the Northern forces. He had distinguished himself as a leader in the United States Army. He was not a slave owner and was personally opposed to slavery. But he was from the state of Virginia. Today, we think of ourselves first as Americans. Then, secondarily, we think of ourselves as citizens of the states where we live. In those days, however, people placed more importance on their state than on the United States. General Lee was a Virginian. He also believed strongly in the con-

Gen. Ullysses S. Grant

cept that states had very strong rights which could not be taken away by the federal government. Therefore, after much "soul searching," he felt honor bound to support his native state of Virginia.

In South Carolina, down in Charleston bay, Ft. Sumter fell to
Southern troops, the war was under way.
The Southern boys took over that island fortress then,
And held it till the war was almost at its end.

The North owned several forts in the Southern states. When the South seceded from the Union, they felt these forts belonged to them since they were on southern property. Of course, the North did not recognize the Confederacy as being a separate country, and they were not about to give up any property to the South.

There was a fort built on an island in the harbor at Charleston, South Carolina. The Confederacy demanded that the Union withdraw from that fort. The Union refused. So on April 12, 1861, the Confederate army fired its guns on Ft. Sumter. It was the beginning of the war. No one at that time had any idea that the war would last a long time or realized how terrible it would be. The South won that first battle and captured Ft. Sumter in Charleston harbor.

In Virginia at Manassas, the first Battle of Bull Run,
The South and North collided, but the Southern army won.
It gave the South much confidence. They thought that they could win.
It made the War much longer than it would have ever been.

The first major confrontation between the armies of the North and the South took place on July 21, 1861, in the state of Virginia near a town named Manassas. The battle took place near a creek called Bull Run. The battle was called the **Battle of Bull Run** in the South and the **Battle of Manassas** in the North.

In general, the South named battles after the nearest body of water, while the North named battles after the towns at which they took place.

The South was the winner at the Battle of Bull Run. (There would later be another battle there, so that first engagement was then referred to as the First Battle of Bull Run.) It proved in later days to be unfortunate that the South won that battle. The South had far less resources with which to fight a war. That victory gave them the confidence they needed to continue the fight. Had they lost the first battles, the war might have ended much sooner.

> *The North had lots of factories for guns and ships and shells.*
> *The South relied on money crops, tobacco, cotton bales.*
> *The Confederates sent to Europe for the armaments of war,*
> *But when the Union blocked their ports, the South received no more.*

From the very start, the North had an enormous advantage in the war. They had farms which grew food in abundance. They had factories in which they could produce their own guns and shells and even heavy artillery. They had a sprawling network of railroads which could transport troops quickly. Finally, in population they had more than twice as many people. The population of the North was 19 million. The population of the South was only 9 million and of these, 3.5 million were slaves.

The South had very few factories. They had to buy their weapons in Europe and transport them on ships. The North knew this very well. So their strategy was to **blockade** the ports of the South to prevent them from importing guns and supplies. That meant that the Northern ships lined up across the ports and prevented ships from entering. Also, the North had many more ships than the South.

> *Not only was it fought on land, but also on the sea.*
> *The South owned the Merrimac; it fought ingeniously.*
> *It clashed with the Monitor, that frigate of the North.*
> *Those ironclad vessels changed the course of naval war.*

In order to break the North's blockade, the South came up with a new idea for naval war. All ships at that time were made of wood. The South took an old ship called the **Merrimac,** and attached heavy steel plates to the outside so that cannon balls could not hurt it. Also, the navy attached a steel ram on the front so that it could run into and pierce enemy ships.

The North had its own shipyards. It also built an ironclad ship called the **Monitor**. When these two ships met in battle, they could not defeat each other. It was a draw. This started a great change in the way ships would be built all over the world. From that time on, men began building ships out of iron.

The Civil War

*In '62, the Union charged the capital of the South
    To cut the railroad lines and knock their major armies out.
Confederate Army soldiers held their capital that day;
    But lost some major battles in old Virgin-i-a.*

After the first battles of the Civil War which took place in 1860, Lincoln wanted to defeat the South, quickly. He thought the best way to do this would be to capture their capital. The **York River** and the **James River** are two rivers which go toward Richmond, Virginia, which was the capital of the Confederacy. The land between Richmond and the Chesapeake Bay forms a peninsula. Therefore, this effort to send troops to capture Richmond was called the **Peninsular Campaign**. While the Union was not successful in reaching Richmond, there was a famous battle fought there called the **Battle of Seven Pines**. The South lost that battle. But that is where Robert E. Lee was first appointed the Commanding General of the Confederate Army.

As noted earlier, the North had a vast network of railroads which could move troops and supplies very quickly. The very first steam locomotives began running in the United States in 1831. The railroad was a relatively new invention, but a very important one for the war effort. The South had far fewer miles of track and far fewer locomotives than the North. By destroying tracks, engines and bridges, the Northern forces could make the logistics of war in the South far more difficult. Had they captured Richmond as planned, they surely would have destroyed the tracks between Richmond and Norfolk. Since Norfolk was an important port city, its railroads were even more important that the ones at the inland city of Richmond. However, since many supplies were funneled out of Richmond, their railroads were also important targets. The city of Peterburg to the south of Richmond was an even more important railroad center. In fact, many people believe that is why General Grand later shifted his base of operations south of Richmond and the James River in 1864.

*The Shenandoah Valley was the path through which they surged
    To a town in Pennsylvania by the name of Gettysburg.
Lee's troops were devastated, were forced into retreat.
    It turned the tide against the South in July of '63.*

The South greatly wanted the support of the European nations from whom they could buy supplies. But the European nations did not want to support a loser. In order for the South to convince the Europeans they were powerful enough to win the war, they felt they had to go into Northern territory and win a major battle there. Most of the battles had been fought in the South. The South actually won many of those battles.

General Lee and Traveler at Gettysburg

For this reason, Lee moved his troops through a large valley that runs between two mountain ranges called the **Shenandoah Valley**. It extends

73

clear up into Pennsylvania to a town called Gettysburg. Here, the battle which is certainly the most famous battle of the Civil War, **The Battle of Gettysburg,** was fought. It lasted for three days. The Union forces won that battle. When it was all over, the South had lost so many men that they could never again find enough troops to successfully defeat the North. That was considered the turning point of the war when the North really took control.

> *On the Mississippi River, the Union troops attacked*
> *To stop the Southern armies and split the South in half.*
> *They captured ol' New Orleans and finally Vicksburg,*
> *And after that, the South was practically deterred.*

While the Battle of Gettysburg was taking place in the Northern states, another very important battle was taking place in the South on the Mississippi River. It was called the **Battle of Vicksburg.** It ended in a victory for the North just one day after the victory at Gettysburg. By winning this battle, the North took control of the Mississippi River so that the South could not ship much needed supplies across the river. Also, that is one of the battles where General Grant became famous. As a result of that, he became Commander of all the Northern forces some time later.

> *Bull Run and Antietam, Cold Harbor, Fredericksburg,*
> *Perryville and Nashville, Stone Harbor, and Vicksburg,*
> *Chattanooga, Chickamauga, Shiloh, Mobile Bay*
> *Were the names of famous battles in our nation's darkest day.*

There were over 2,000 different battles in the Civil War. Some were huge confrontations involving more than 100,000 men. Others were small skirmishes fought by only a few people.

Lincoln's Gettysburg Address

In the final year of war, Grant fought furiously;
He captured Virginia and finally Tennessee.
In the state of Alabama, he captured Mobile Bay,
And when he routed Nashville, the end was on its way.

After losing Gettysburg and Vicksburg, the South would never have a good chance to win the war, but they kept on fighting. A number of battles were fought which allowed the North to capture several Southern states. Grant was now firmly in control of the Northern army.

In the Battle of Atlanta, Gen'ral Sherman with his might,
Destroyed that Southern city, ravaged everything in sight.
He marched on to Savannah, burning cities, fields, and inns.
That's why they say that Georgia, then, was gone with the wind.

In spite of the fact that the South could not raise enough men or guns to win the war, they still would not quit. General Grant knew the only way to make them stop was to totally devastate the land and the people. Grant sent another famous general, General William T. Sherman, to destroy the Southern army in South Carolina and Georgia. As Sherman's troops swept through the South, they not only defeated the weakened troops of the Confederacy, they burned the cities and the fields, destroying the crops. There was much starvation and misery. A famous book was written almost a century later called "Gone With the Wind," which described the devastation and destruction that occurred. The old way of life in the South was truly destroyed by General Sherman who swept through like a destructive windstorm.

General Sherman

When Grant captured Richmond in 1865,
The Southern troops were finished; Lee could not survive.
At a place called Appomattox in Virginia, one day,
The Confederacy surrendered, and the South was held at bay.

Finally, after the Southern army was in shambles, Grant took control of the capital of the South, Richmond, Virginia. Lee knew they could not fight any longer. He surrendered to General Grant on April 9, 1865. Very shortly thereafter, all the other Southern generals surrendered also. Finally, the war was over.

Study Questions:

1. Why would the people of the Northern States have been less concerned about slavery than the people in the Southern States?

2. Why do you think the leaders in both the North and the South considered it important to preserve the Union (keep the States united) before the Civil War?

3. If the people of a territory had the right to join the Union, why shouldn't they have had the right to leave the union?

4. Why would the people of the North have cared whether the Southern states went their own way or not?

5. It was generally thought by the leaders of both the North and the South that the War between the States would not be a long, drawn-out affair, but that the outcome would be determined by a few short, but very decisive battles. Why do you think they were wrong about this?

6. Suppose that early in the War, the South had achieved their objective of capturing Washington, D.C., and defeating the Union Army, thus winning an early victory. How would this have changed life in America?

7. Had they known that the war would continue for four years and that over 600,000 soldiers would die, do you think they would have pursued the fighting? Why or why not?

8. What other alternatives other than war might they have had?

9. Why do you think the Confederates felt that nations like England and France would come to their aid during the war?

10. Toward the end of the War, President Lincoln ordered massive destruction in the South, which was carried out by General Sherman. This caused great suffering to ordinary people, both white and black. Why did President Lincoln think it was necessary to destroy the towns and farms, including the burning of the crops?

11. Was it right for President Lincoln to do this? Would it ever be right for a President to order wartime destruction on non-soldiers in order to accomplish a noble purpose of peace? Can you think of any other times when this was done?

12. Why do you think the South held on and fought so furiously even when the possibility of victory had passed?

Reconstruction

About the music...
(Tape 2, Song 2)

Reconstruction was a sad time in American history. Even though the slaves were free, their lives were not greatly gladdened by the events that took place in the South. Though there were some hopeful times, no one was really satisfied. The music, therefore, is minor or doleful in tone.

The instruments you hear predominantly are the jazz piano, the bass fiddle, and percussion or drums. You might describe this as a jazz ensemble.

When the Civil War was over in 1865,
   The Union was divided, the South did not survive.
Reconstruction was the process to reunite the states
   That freedom, law and justice might again perpetuate.

Chorus

Reconstruction, after the Civil War
   When the states were reunited and the South would rise no more.

Reconstruction started in 1865.
   The process took twelve years, though few were satisfied.
By 1877, the process found its end
   When th' eleven Southern states were all admitted once again.

In '63, Lincoln had a plan he would enact;
   Said the South was in rebellion, but their statehood was intact.
He proposed an oath of loyalty for 10 percent or more;
   Declared that when this number signed, their rights would be restored.

Chorus

The Republicans in Congress were angry with this plan,
   Felt the South should be well punished for their having left the land.
They wanted them considered as foreign, conquered states who would
   Have to do much more before they could repatriate.

On the 14th day of April in 1865,
    Lincoln then was murdered, and his plan did not survive.
Andrew Johnson became President, and it was his to guide
    This nation through those years when very few were satisfied.

Chorus

Well the Northern states survived the war with property intact,
    But the South had been destroyed by Union armies' fierce attack.
Cities, railroads, houses, crops and factories were void.
    The economy and government were totally destroyed.

The biggest change of all was that the slaves, at last, were free.
    They left the old plantations to experience liberty.
But they had no jobs or property to support them or their kin.
    Former masters had no money to employ them once again.

Chorus

The Freedmen's Bureau formed to aid the devastated South.
    Started hospitals and schools, and handed food and clothing out.
It also had a court system to handle those disputes
    'Tween former slaves and masters, true justice to impute.

Andrew Johnson re-established Southern governments just when
    The Confed'rates agreed to swear allegiance once again.
The power was returned to white planters as before;
    Former slaves were still oppressed in this newly caused uproar.

Chorus

Well Congress overturned Johnson's Reconstruction plan.
    They refused to accept the new Southern congressmen;
Passed the Fourteenth Amendment to grant equal rights and votes
    To blacks as well as whites and to all the common folk.

The Republican Congress passed the Reconstruction Acts
    Which abolished Southern rule formed under Andrew Johnson's pacts.
They registered black voters and formed mixed governments.
    The Congress controlled everything which was their full intent.

Chorus

Reconstruction

The Congress of the Northern states was firmly in control.
　They commanded Southern states new constitutions to unfold.
They sent the Northern army to enforce their stricter laws.
　A social revolution in the South it surely caused.

This new day in the South seemed too good to survive.
　Blacks and whites in government walked truly side by side.
Black mayors, legislators, teachers, congressmen,
　Had rights they'd never dreamed of when they'd been the slaves of men.

Chorus

The carpetbaggers came to take advantage of the South.
　Politicians, teachers, businessmen who the Northern cause espoused.
They set up southern governments that were friendly to the North.
　They were hated by the South who tried to throw them out by force.

Racial violence increased throughout the angry Southern lands.
　They formed their white militias such as the Ku Klux Klan.
They used intimidation to prevent the new black vote.
　It took lots of Northern arms to keep those governments afloat.

Chorus

In '69, the Fifteenth Amendment was in place.
　States could not deny the right to vote because of race.
This was the most important of the Reconstruction laws.
　It formed the base of Civil Rights in future freedoms' cause.

The cost of reconstruction was a burden to the North;
　Supporting occupation armies was a most expensive course;
In 1876, Southern home rule was returned.
　The vic'tries of the last ten years were gone to all concerned.

Chorus

Reconstruction was a failure almost from the start.
　The benefits of freedom, they just could not impart.
But men must keep on trying always through the years,
　To erase hate and injustice and wipe away the tears.

Chorus

Reconstruction Song

"With malice toward none; with charity for all; with firmness in the right, as God gives us to see the right, let us strive on to finish the work we are in; to bind up the nation's wounds; to care for him who shall have borne the battle, and for his widow, and his orphan—to do all which may achieve and cherish a just and lasting peace among ourselves, and with all nations."
— Abraham Lincoln. Second Inaugural, March 4, 1865

"The war being at an end, the Southern states having laid down their arms, and the questions at issue between them and the Northern states having been decided, I believe it to be the duty of everyone to unite in the restoration of the country and the re-establishment of peace and harmony."
— General Robert E. Lee

When the Civil War was over in 1865,
    the Union was divided, the South did not survive.
Reconstruction was the process to reunite the states
    That freedom, law and justice might again perpetuate.

The most tragic period of American history was, without a doubt, the Civil War. 620,000 American soldiers died in that enormous conflict. Worst of all, they were not fighting against some sinister foreign enemy. They were fighting against other Americans. Sometimes members of the same family were fighting on opposite sides.

The war was waged to keep the South in the Union. When the war was over, the South was, indeed, a part of the Union, but they did not have the same rights as the States in the North. They had no representatives in Congress. The people had no voting rights.

Should the eleven Southern states who had seceded immediately take their place again as independent sovereign states? Would they once again take up their privileges as though nothing had happened? Would they have to prove their worthiness to re-enter the Union? What would be the process to heal the wounds and re-establish the United States of America?

The period of time during which the Southern states were to re-establish themselves is called **Reconstruction**. As the war ended and Reconstruction began, there were many different ideas as to how this process should take place.

Reconstruction

Reconstruction started in 1865.
The process took twelve years, though few were satisfied.
By 1877, the process found its end
When th' eleven Southern states were all admitted once again.

Immediately after the South surrendered, Reconstruction began. It was a process that would last for twelve difficult years. Some Northern political leaders wanted to punish the Southern states severely. Others felt the process should be an easy and merciful one. It began in 1865 and ended in 1877. The end did not come because a satisfactory resolution and agreement had been reached. Indeed, the opposite was the case. The North simply grew weary of the process and became too burdened with its own problems. In essence, they gave up on Reconstruction.

Andrew Johnson

In '63, Lincoln had a plan he would enact;
Said the South was in rebellion, but their statehood was intact.
He proposed an oath of loyalty for 10 percent or more;
Declared that when this number signed, their rights would be restored.

Abraham Lincoln was President of the United States during the Civil War. He was also President when it ended. He had a plan for Reconstruction which would have been very merciful to the South and very easy for them to accomplish. He proposed that if at least ten percent of the men in a Southern state would sign an oath of loyalty to the United States, their statehood would be restored with all the rights and privileges that other states enjoyed. This would have been easy for every state to accomplish.

The Republicans in Congress were angry with this plan,
Felt the South should be well punished for their having left the land.
They wanted them considered as foreign, conquered states who would
Have to do much more before they could repatriate.

Lincoln's ideas were not popular with all of the people in Congress, however. The Republican Party had most of the seats in Congress during the Civil War, and most of the Republicans thought the Southern states should be punished for their rebellion against the nation. They thought the people of the South should be forced to pay large amounts of money called **reparations** as punishment. They thought the Southern states should be treated no differently than a foreign country who might have attacked the United States.

On the 14th day of April in 1865,
Lincoln then was murdered, and his plan did not survive.
Andrew Johnson became President, and it was his to guide
This nation through those years when very few were satisfied.

Unfortunately, President Lincoln would never see his plan put into effect. Just a very few days after the war was over, President Lincoln was assassinated while attending the theater in Washington. As specified in the Constitution, the Vice-President, a man named **Andrew Johnson**, became President.

Andrew Johnson was actually from the South, from the state of Tennessee. However, he had remained loyal to the Union. It would be much more difficult for him to enact a Reconstruction plan since he did not enjoy the same support from Congress as did Abraham Lincoln.

> *Well the Northern states survived the war with property intact,*
> *But the South had been destroyed by Union armies' fierce attack.*
> *Cities, railroads, houses, crops and factories were void.*
> *The economy and government were totally destroyed.*

At the end of the war, there were many changes in the country. The Northern states had lost many soldiers, but their property was still intact because almost all of the fighting and destruction had taken place in the South. Their factories were running. Their railroads were running. Their cities had hardly been affected at all.

The situation was quite different in the South, however. Almost all of the great battles had been fought there. In the process of winning the war, the Northern Army destroyed the railroads, the highways, and the bridges. They also had burned many towns. They had even burned up fields of crops as well as the farm houses. As long as the people of the South had food and money, they would not stop making war. For this reason, the North felt they had no choice. Either they had to destroy property in this way, or the war would continue for a longer period of time.

In addition to the property being destroyed, their means of earning money was also destroyed. They had no money. They had spent almost all of it on the war effort. Also they had no laborers since the slaves had been freed. The huge plantations of the South required many, many workers. Without slave labor, the work could not be done. With no money, they could not hire laborers to do the work.

> *The biggest change of all was that the slaves, at last, were free.*
> *They left the old plantations to experience liberty.*
> *But they had no jobs or property to support them or their kin.*
> *Former masters had no money to employ them once again.*

The slaves were free. They had actually received their freedom when Abraham Lincoln made his famous **Emancipation Proclamation** during the Civil War. But they did not realize their freedom until the South was defeated in the War. So the former slaves were free to leave the plantations and go wherever they wished. But where could they go? Their former white masters had no money to pay them and did not wish to pay them anyway. They couldn't really go to the North, for while the people of the North desired emancipation in the South, they didn't desire equality for black people in their own states. They did not want them competing for jobs in those regions. So while the Union states opposed slavery, white people there were actually no more free of prejudice and bigotry than those in the South.

> *The Freedmen's Bureau formed to aid the devastated South.*
> *Started hospitals and schools, and handed food and clothing out.*
> *It also had a court system to handle those disputes*
> *'Tween former slaves and masters, true justice to impute.*

Because of the great needs, particularly among former slaves, a government agency called the **Freedmen's Bureau** was formed by Congress. At this time, there were no state governments in the South. Military commanders from the North were in charge of the states. The Freedmen's Bureau started schools for the black people. In most states, education had been denied to blacks. For the first time, they began to learn to read and write. The people also had great physical needs. So hospitals were started to meet those needs.

It was very difficult at that time for black people to receive justice in their disputes, particularly with their former masters. Therefore, the Freedmen's Bureau appointed judges to handle those disputes as justly as they could.

> *Andrew Johnson re-established Southern governments just when*
> *The Confed'rates agreed to swear allegiance once again.*
> *The power was returned to white planters as before;*
> *Former slaves were still oppressed in this newly caused uproar.*

President Johnson was now in charge of Reconstruction. He decided to pardon all Southerners who would sign an oath of loyalty to the United States except for the main leaders of the Confederacy and many of the wealthy Southern families. He then allowed the states to form new governments provided they would outlaw slavery and swear allegiance to the United States. In the fall of 1865, theses new state governments were organized. However, Johnson made no provision for giving blacks a right to vote or protecting their rights. The state governments were to make these decisions themselves.

As soon as these new state governments formed, they immediately began to oppress the blacks by passing laws called **Black Codes**. Under these laws, blacks could be treated almost as harshly as they were in the days of slavery.

> *Well Congress overturned Johnson's Reconstruction plan.*
> *They refused to accept the new Southern congressmen;*
> *Passed the Fourteenth Amendment to grant equal rights and votes*
> *To blacks as well as whites and to all the common folk.*

The Republican Congress passed the Reconstruction Acts
Which abolished Southern rule formed under Andrew Johnson's pacts.
They registered black voters and formed mixed governments.
The Congress controlled everything which was their full intent.

In late 1865, when Congress returned from the summer and fall recess, Congressmen and Senators from the Southern states came to claim their seats under the provisions of President Johnson's reconstruction plan. This plan had been put into effect during the summer and fall recess of the Congress. Many of these new Southern members of the House and the Senate had been office holders in the Confederacy. The Congress was controlled by the Republicans from the North and they refused to seat the new members of Congress from the South. That means they would not allow them to participate or vote in the Congress.

When the members of Congress learned of the new state governments in the South created under President Johnson's Reconstruction Plan, and when they heard about the Black Codes, they decided that the President's Plan did not work. When they refused to seat the new Congressmen from the South, they also decided that the Congress, not the President, should enact the plan for Reconstruction.

The Congress did three things that year concerning Reconstruction. First, they passed a law called the **Civil Rights Act** which gave former slaves legal rights. Then, they passed the **Fourteenth Amendment** to the Constitution which made all black people citizens and required all federal and state laws to be applied equally to blacks and whites. The third thing they did was to pass a group of laws called the **Reconstruction Acts**.

The Reconstruction Acts said the state governments formed under President Andrew Johnson's reconstruction plan were no longer legal or valid. That meant that all of the governors and legislators elected under those new governments could not hold office. Instead, they divided the South into five regions and placed army generals in control. Still other laws required that election boards be formed to register voters, making sure that all black males were registered to vote. Another provision was that the new voters in the states would form state constitutional conventions which must ratify the Fourteenth Amendment.

President Johnson opposed the Reconstruction Acts. When he tried to fire certain government officials whose job it was to enforce these new laws, he was **impeached** by the House of Representatives. That means the Congress tried to remove him from his office as President of the United States. When a President is impeached by the House of Representatives, that does not mean that he is removed from office. He must then be put on trial by the U.S. Senate. In that trial, the Senate voted not to remove him from office. The vote to remove him from office fell short by just one vote.

> *The Congress of the Northern states was firmly in control.*
> *They commanded Southern states new constitutions to unfold.*
> *They sent the Northern army to enforce their stricter laws.*
> *A social revolution in the South it surely caused.*

Now the Congress was in control of Reconstruction, not the President of the United States. They also controlled the Army. The Congress had the support and the votes of the blacks in the South. Therefore, the new state governments and constitutions were written to insure that black citizens had an equal voice. The white voters opposed these new changes, but they were outnumbered and could not resist the Army governors who were in control.

> *This new day in the South seemed too good to survive.*
> *Blacks and whites in government walked truly side by side.*
> *Black mayors, legislators, teachers, congressmen,*
> *Had rights they'd never dreamed of when they'd been the slaves of men.*

An amazing thing happened beginning in 1867. Under the new state governments approved under Congress's Reconstruction Plan, blacks truly had full rights in the South. There were black men elected to public offices. Some were mayors, some became state legislators, and some were elected to Congress. Nothing like this had ever happened before. But this could only last as long as the Northern army was in control of the South.

> *The carpetbaggers came to take advantage of the South.*
> *Politicians, teachers, businessmen who the Northern cause espoused.*
> *They set up southern governments that were friendly to the North.*
> *They were hated by the South who tried to throw them out by force.*

The whites in the South violently opposed the new state governments. They hated the people from the North who came to rule over them. They called them "**carpetbaggers.**" This name came from the type of suitcases that were common in that day called carpetbags. These Northerners came to the South for many reasons. Some wanted to accomplish truly good things for the people. There were teachers who taught in the new black schools. There were nurses who worked in the hospitals which were set up.

Others came for reasons that were not so noble. They were businessmen who knew they could take advantage of the people in those states where many local businesses had been destroyed, and the local businessmen had no money to re-open their businesses.

Others were politicians who knew they could either be elected or appointed to political office as long as the Northern army was in control of the region. Some of these politicians were good men while others were very corrupt and dishonest.

Because many of the Southerners had been denied the right to vote by the occupation army from the North, and because blacks did have the right to vote, mixed governments were set up. These governments did a number of good things such as establishing schools, rebuilding roads, and guaranteeing civil rights to blacks. However, they did not have the support of the white population in the South, and they could only survive as long as armed soldiers from the North were there to protect them. They were even opposed by some blacks who objected to the rule of white Northern politicians in places where they felt black office holders would be more appropriate.

> *Racial violence increased throughout the angry Southern lands.*
> *They formed their white militias such as the Ku Klux Klan.*
> *They used intimidation to prevent the new black vote.*
> *It took lots of Northern arms to keep those governments afloat.*

As opposition increased, violence increased in the South. There were terrible race riots where many people were killed. Groups such as the Ku Klux Klan were formed. These groups would dress in white robes and hoods and commit acts of violence against blacks. They even threatened blacks to keep them from participating in elections. The only protection available was from the Northern armies who were acting as policemen in the South. But the South was much too big a place to police. There were not enough soldiers to do the job.

Ku Klux Klan

What was the objective of the North in reconstruction? Was justice their main intent? Perhaps this was the case in the minds of many people. But the Republican Party of that day also had other motives. They wanted to use the South to maintain their power in the nation. They knew they could count on the new voters of the South for votes. So they passed laws which would make it difficult for the Democratic Party to regain power. Blacks were not welcomed with job opportunities in the Northern states anymore than they were in the South. Neither were they given the right to vote in the North when those rights were guaranteed in the South.

> *In '69, the Fifteenth Amendment was in place.*
> *States could not deny the right to vote because of race.*
> *This was the most important of the Reconstruction laws.*
> *It formed the base of Civil Rights in future freedoms' cause.*

Reconstruction

Perhaps one of the most important and lasting things that happened during Reconstruction was the passing of the **Fifteenth Amendment** to the Constitution. This made it illegal for any state to deny the right to vote because of race. While other laws of Reconstruction were either abandoned or overturned in later years, the Fifteenth Amendment remained. Other Civil Rights laws which would be passed years and even decades later were made possible by the Fifteenth Amendment to the Constitution.

> *The cost of Reconstruction was a burden to the North;*
> *Supporting occupation armies was a most expensive course.*
> *In 1876, Southern home rule was returned*
> *The vic'tries of the last ten years were gone to all concerned.*

Rutherford B. Hayes

Who paid the salaries of the soldiers who occupied the South? The money came from taxes paid by U.S. citizens. The citizens of the North had to pay these high taxes. The states of Tennessee and Virginia had been re-admitted to the Union by 1870. In those states, the Democratic Party had regained power over the state governments in spite of the efforts of the Republican Party to keep them out of power. Throughout the South, the Democrats also regained control of the state legislatures. That means that the voters elected Democrats to the state Houses of Representatives and the state Senates.

The people of the North became weary of paying taxes to support Reconstruction. Also, as the Southern states were gradually accepted back into the Union, it became obvious that the North would have little future control in the South.

Samuel J. Tilden

Reconstruction came to an end as a result of the presidential election of 1876. **Rutherford B. Hayes**, a Republican, was running against **Samuel J. Tilden**, a Democrat. When all the votes were counted, the election was still in doubt. The outcome of the election depended on the votes of three states in the South which still had Reconstruction governments—Florida, Louisiana, and South Carolina. A compromise was made in those states which allowed the Republican, Rutherford Hayes, to be elected. The support of the states was given to him. In return, he agreed to withdraw all federal troops and allow those states to be readmitted to the Union.

Reconstruction was a failure almost from the start.
The benefits of freedom, they just could not impart.
But men must keep on trying always through the years,
To erase hate and injustice and wipe away the tears.

Reconstruction was a dark and sad period in American history. It's purpose was to reunite the states which had left the union so that this nation would once again be harmonious and the people of the states united in a spirit of brotherhood.

This was almost impossible after a bitter Civil War in which 620,000 soldiers died. It was made more difficult by the fact that Southerners also lost much of their property. The emancipation of the slaves left the black people without any source of income. Neither did they have any rights as citizens. Not only were they displaced in the South, but they were not welcome in the North. Great political differences also divided the nation. The North was not about to share any ruling power with the Southern states.

Hatred divided the people of this nation. Abraham Lincoln, the one President who might have been able to bring the people together, had been murdered right at the beginning of Reconstruction. The new President, Andrew Johnson, was a Southerner who could not get along with the Congress. In that regard, Reconstruction was doomed to failure from the very beginning.

During Reconstruction, there were some years when some very real progress was made for black Americans. Schools were set up so that they began receiving education. They were given the right to vote and even had the power to exercise their votes.

Those gains, however, did not last very long. Indeed, after Reconstruction, when the Southern states took over their own governments, most of the rights the black Americans had gained were denied once again.

The two points of progress which remained were the Fourteenth and Fifteenth Amendments to the Constitution. Even though the rights and freedoms of black Americans were abused through the years, these amendments insured that they were, indeed, citizens and that their rights were guaranteed. In later years, the Civil Rights movement was built upon these great amendments.

Even today, the effects of the Civil War are not gone. There is still a certain amount of hostility between the Northern and Southern states. Racial hatred has not disappeared.

It is important for every person to work to create a country where people are accepted, an acceptance not based upon the color of their skin or from which country their parents come. We need a country where everyone has the right to life, liberty and the pursuit of happiness guaranteed by the Constitution of the United States of America.

Study Questions:

1. After the Civil War, Abraham Lincoln's plan allowed that a state could be readmitted to the Union if only 10% of its citizens would sign an oath of loyalty to the United States. Do you think he was being too lenient? What would you have required for a state to have its privileges returned?

2. Why did so many Northern Congressmen want to make re-entry into the Union very difficult for the Southern states?

3. Do you think life was more or less difficult for the slaves immediately after they were emancipated? Explain.

4 During Reconstruction, black people were granted the right to vote in the South but not in all the Northern states. Why do you think the Northern legislators failed to grant voting right in their own states?

5. Racial reform in the South worked only as long as the Northern army was there to enforce the laws. What do you think motivated the Northern-controlled Congress to keep paying the enormous costs of having soldiers stay in the South?

6. When the Northern armies were withdrawn from the South, the white leaders took control of the government just as before the War. Why was Reconstruction a failure?

Amendment freeing the slaves

Go West, Young Man

About the music...
(Tape 2, Song3)

This music is done in a western ballad style. You will hear the instruments of a western band including the "jazz" piano, the guitar, the fiddle, the bass fiddle and, of course, the drums and percussion. A flute is also heard carrying the melody or tune of the song.

Because the growth of the nation portrayed in this song is a happy and cheerful thing, it is played in a major key to a snappy beat.

When the United States was born, there were thirteen states
gathered on the great Atlantic Ocean shore.
There was a great expanse yet to cultivate over at this
brand new nation's western door.

These lands were claimed by England, France and Spain,
but were occupied by Indian nation tribes.
A land of forests, rivers, deserts, mountains and the western plains
where the buffalo and wild life once did thrive.

Chorus

Go west, young man, to a bright and shining land.
You will find a brand new start with a song upon your heart
Perseverance is the key, as you live expectantly
In this land of golden opportunity.

When they spoke of the West in those early days,
they meant Kentucky, Indiana, Tennessee.
Pioneers like Daniel Boone blazed a wilderness trail
thro' the lands of tribal Indians and trees.

The Northwest Territory was a conquest grand
of the Revolutionary War.
Ohio, Indiana, Illinois and Michigan
was the farthest west that men had gone before.

Chorus

Congress passed the Northwest Ordinance Act
    before the 1800's had begun.
It ensured that governments of these vast new lands
    by U.S. law and justice would be run.

In the year eighteen four, an expedition was sent out
    to explore those uncharted western lands.
They sailed the rivers, crossed the mountains where the Indians did roam
    'til they reached the great Pacific Ocean sands.

Chorus

Louisiana was a land that was owned by France. They received it in a treaty
    made with Spain
The Mississippi River ran along that great expanse. It was the highway
    for our produce and our grain.

From the Mississippi River on the eastern side
    to the slopes of Rocky Mountains' eastern face,
From New Orleans to Canada, a giant land. Fifteen
    states would later occupy this space.

Chorus

Napoleon was the ruler of land of France,
    and to conquer Europe was his major goal.
So he sold Louisiana back in eighteen three
    for the money that would furnish his bankroll.

Florida was owned by the land of Spain. It was a land
    of warlike Indians and thieves.
It was a base where hostile forces could attack our states
    and a problem that our leaders must relieve.

Chorus

In 1819, our Congress made a deal,
    and it bought the territory back from Spain.
It secured our southern border with U.S. control
    and restored some law and order once again.

Well, the southwest part of this vast and spacious land
　　was owned by the king and queen of Spain.
Including California, Texas from the mighty Rio Grande
　　to the mountains and the western desert plains.

Chorus

Mexico took over back in 1821
　　when the Spaniards were defeated and expelled.
They feared the Texans would take over just as they had done,
　　so they tried these brand new settlers to repel.

The Texas Revolution came in 1836
　　at the Alamo where Texans nobly died.
But their struggles were avenged on the San Jacinto plains
　　where the fledgling Texas Army turned the tide.

Chorus

The importance of this battle, do not underestimate.
　　The impact of the conflict must be known.
For it meant that all or portions of the western states,
　　th' United States would ultimately own.

When Texas joined the Union back in 1845,
　　a new conflict with Mexico began.
Mexico did claim much of Texas property,
　　and said the border was not the Rio Grande.

Chorus

War was declared back in 1846
　　and the battles did continue two long years.
In the treaty, on the map, California and Utah,
　　Arizona and Nevada did appear.

With the Gadsden Purchase in 1853,
　　the southern border took its final shape.
We bought that strip of land so a railroad one day
　　might be able to cross the southern states.

Chorus

The northwest lands in those early Western days
    were by England and the U.S. jointly shared.
But after settlers headed West on the Oregon Trail,
    a negotiated border was prepared.

That, my friend, tells the story how the West was won
    in the eighteenth and the nineteenth centuries.
How Americans conquered this great expanse
    and established it from sea to shining sea.

Chorus

Daniel Boone sees Kentucky

Go West, Young Man

"Go west, young man, and grow up with the country."
- Horace Greely, Editor, The New York Tribune

When the United States was born, there were thirteen states
gathered on the great Atlantic Ocean shore.
There was a great expanse yet to cultivate over at this
brand new nation's western door.

These lands were claimed by England, France and Spain,
but were occupied by Indian nation tribes.
A land of forests, rivers, deserts, mountains and the western plains
where the buffalo and wild life once did thrive.

At the end of the Revolutionary War, the United States and England conducted peace negotiations in Paris, France. France and Spain also participated in those negotiations. These were the countries who owned most of the lands in North America.

Those negotiations produced a treaty called the **Treaty of Paris**. This treaty recognized the independence of the United States. It also established the borders of the United States.

One of the places that was disputed during the colonial days was Florida. England had claimed Florida in the 1500's inasmuch as it claimed all of the land of North America. Spain had also claimed Florida in the 1500's. There is something more important, however, than merely claiming a territory. Spain actually occupied the land of Florida. The treaty established that Britain gave up her rights to Florida and agreed that Spain owned that land.

The nations recognized in 1883 that the United States owned the land from Canada to Florida as far west as the Mississippi River. Spain owned Florida and the known land to the West of the Mississippi River. This did not really include areas such as Wyoming, Washington, Oregon, the Dakotas, Nebraska, etc. Little was known about these lands. In fact, very few white men had even been to these places.

Shortly after the year 1800, Americans decided it was time to know more about their own land, and the rest of the North American Continent.

When they spoke of the West in those early days,
*   they meant Kentucky, Indiana, Tennessee.*
Pioneers like Daniel Boone blazed a wilderness trail
*   thro' the lands of tribal Indians and trees.*

When we talk about the West today, we think of places like California, Oregon, Colorado, and even Texas. In 1800, no one even thought about places so far away. They considered the West to be anything west of the original thirteen colonies. Even Pittsburgh, Pennsylvania, was considered to be part of the West because it was on the other side of the Allegheny Mountains. In those days, the places we now call Ohio, Kentucky, Tennessee, Indiana and Illinois were all considered to be the West. We now call this part of the country the **Midwest**.

Even before the American Revolution, men began exploring the West. The legendary pioneer, Daniel Boone, began to explore the wilderness of Kentucky and to establish settlements there. It was a dangerous land. The Indians did not take kindly to having white men coming in. The white men built forts for protection against the Indians.

The Northwest Territory was a conquest grand
*   of the Revolutionary War.*
Ohio, Indiana, Illinois and Michigan
*   was the farthest west that men had gone before.*

Congress passed the Northwest Ordinance Act
*   before the 1800's had begun.*
It ensured that governments of these vast new lands
*   by U.S. law and justice would be run.*

Congress knew that people would want to move to the Northwest Territory to take advantage of the good land that was available. Therefore, they passed a law called the **Northwest Ordinance Act of 1787**. This made it possible for settlers to buy land for $1.00 an acre in the new territory.

Moving west was no easy matter. They traveled over rugged trails in covered wagons. They bought flatboats and traveled by river. The further west they went, the greater the danger of attack by Indians.

Why would people venture west with danger like that? Some wanted land of their own, but could not afford it in the eastern states. Some, like Daniel Boone and other explorers, simply wanted to taste adventure. After all, their forefathers had taken even greater risks when they came from Europe to settle the New World. These people had the same adventuresome spirit. Newspapers of the day told of the opportunities and urged people with words such as, "Go West Young Man."

In the years to come, the territories had enough people to apply for statehood. By 1803, the states of Vermont, Kentucky, Tennessee, and Ohio had been added to the Union. Soon other states such as Indiana, Illinois, Michigan, and Wisconsin would be added.

> *In the year eighteen four, an expedition was sent out*
> *to explore those uncharted western lands.*
> *They sailed the rivers, crossed the mountains where the Indians did roam*
> *'til they reached the great Pacific Ocean sands.*

Thomas Jefferson became President of the United States in 1801. Very little was known about the Louisiana Territory. The President wanted to find a land route to the Pacific Ocean so that trade could be started to the Far East.

Even the earliest expeditions to the New World sought to find such a trade route. That was Christopher Columbus' objective in 1492. In fact, when he reached **The West Indies**, he thought he had reached India. That is why he called the people "Indians," and why we refer to native Americans as Indians to this day.

In 1804, President Jefferson sent an expedition to explore the Louisiana Territory. They were to draw maps and describe the features of the land, the vegetation and the animals in great detail. They were to make friends with the Indians and establish good relations with them so that other men could safely travel over the land. The leaders of the 45-man expedition were **Captain Merriwether Lewis** and **Captain William Clark**. The expedition became known as the **Lewis and Clark Expedition**. Their travels lasted two years.

Meriwether Lewis   William Clark

They sailed up the Mississippi River, then up the Missouri River. They crossed the beautiful snow-capped Rocky Mountains. Then they traveled down to the Columbia River and finally reached the Pacific coast. As a result of their mapping that area, the United States claimed the Oregon Territory. In future years, thousands of settlers would brave the wilderness and travel to Oregon.

> *Louisiana was a land that was owned by France. They received it*
> > *in a treaty made with Spain*
> *The Mississippi River ran along that great expanse. It was the highway*
> > *for our produce and our grain.*
>
> *From the Mississippi River on the eastern side*
> > *to the slopes of Rocky Mountains' eastern face,*
> *From New Orleans to Canada, a giant land. Fifteen states*
> > *would later occupy this space.*
>
> *Napoleon was the ruler of land of France,*
> > *and to conquer Europe was his major goal.*
> *So he sold Louisiana back in eighteen three*
> > *for the money that would furnish his bankroll.*

After the Revolutionary War, it was agreed that the territory called Louisiana was owned by Spain. Twenty years after the Treaty of Paris was signed, in 1803, Spain made an agreement with France and gave them the Louisiana Territory. The Mississippi River was the border between the United States and Louisiana.

One of the most important cities on the North American Continent was the city of **New Orleans** at the mouth of the Mississippi River on the Gulf of Mexico. President Jefferson knew it was very important that the United States own that city so ships coming down the Mississippi River could have access to the Gulf of Mexico and the rest of the world. If New Orleans were controlled by a foreign country and that country should become the enemy of the United States, boat traffic and trade from the states bordering that enormous river could be totally stopped. In those days, there were no roads or railroads. The great rivers were the only highways on which great quantities of goods could be shipped.

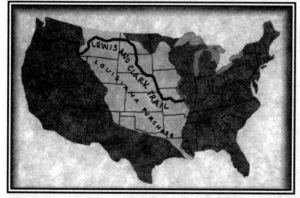

After Spain granted Louisiana to France, President Jefferson offered to buy New Orleans for $2 million. The ruler of France at the time was a famous general named **Napoleon**. He was trying to conquer all of Europe. Enormous amounts of money were required to support his army and buy the weapons he needed. America was far, far away from Europe, and he reasoned that he needed money more than he needed unexplored land in the distant American wilderness. Therefore, he sold all of the Louisiana Territory to the United States for $15 million. In those days, that was an enormous amount of money, but it allowed the United States to double the size of the country. All, or part, of fifteen large states would one day occupy this territory.

> *Florida was owned by the land of Spain. It was a land*
> *of warlike Indians and thieves.*
> *It was a base where hostile forces could attack our states*
> *and a problem that our leaders must relieve.*

The Treaty of Paris after the Revolutionary War granted the land of **Florida** to the nation of Spain. England had actually owned Florida between the years of 1763 and 1781. The Spaniards marched in and occupied Florida during the Revolutionary War when the British were unable to defend it because their troops were occupied fighting the Americans. The peace treaty then made it official that Spain owned Florida.

Spain, however, did not rule Florida well. She refused to do what was necessary to maintain law and order. She did not send police there to punish criminals. For this reason, prisoners, criminals and thieves of all kinds moved to Florida where they could do their evil deeds without being punished.

These evil people did not simply stay in Florida. They would roam into the colony of Georgia and raid the farms and property of Americans, then run back to Florida where they could escape law and justice.

> *In 1819, our Congress made a deal*
> *and it bought the territory back from Spain.*
> *It secured our southern border with U.S. control*
> *and restored some law and order once again.*

In 1819, after the War of 1812 was completely over, the United States made a treaty with Spain and purchased Florida for $5 million. The money, however, was not paid to Spain. Instead, it was paid to the Americans who had been robbed and victimized because Spain had refused to maintain law and order in Florida.

After the United States took over and sent in Federal marshals and troops to rid the territory of criminals, many American settlers moved to Florida to start new lives there.

> *Well, the southwest part of this vast and spacious land*
> *was owned by the king and queen of Spain.*
> *Including California, Texas from the mighty Rio Grande*
> *to the mountains and the western desert plains.*

The land, which is now the Southwest part of the United States, was almost totally unoccupied by white men in 1800. It was a land run by Indian tribes, as it had been for centuries and centuries. The Spaniards had many missions throughout the land where they taught the Indians their religion and culture, but there were almost no settlers.

> *Mexico took over back in 1821*
> *when the Spaniards were defeated and expelled.*
> *They feared the Texans would take over just as they had done,*
> *so they tried these brand new settlers to repel.*

General Sam Houston

In 1821, the people of Mexico wanted independence from Spain. They were tired of having Spaniards ruling over them. The Spaniards removed the gold, silver and other great wealth from Mexico and treated the people badly. The Mexicans fought and won a war of independence against Spain, and established Mexico as a separate country.

The nation of Mexico owned all of what is Mexico today, and all of the land that is now Texas, New Mexico, Arizona and most of California. Though they owned the land, they did not occupy very much of it. They wanted settlers to occupy the land. But it was a long way from where most of the people of Mexico lived. Mexicans did not want to move that far away from their own people. So Mexico invited Americans to come and buy land very inexpensively and become Mexican citizens. Thousands of Americans went to Texas, bought land and established farms, ranches, and towns.

By about 1830, there were more Americans in Texas than there were Mexicans. Then in 1833, a dictator named **Santa Ana** took control of Mexico. He was afraid the Americans in Texas would rebel against Mexico. After all, hadn't the Mexicans rebelled against their Spanish rulers just twelve years earlier? Americans were different than Mexicans. American culture was like English culture, while Mexicans had a combination of Spanish and Indian culture. Therefore, the Mexican government stopped the immigration of Americans and began to limit the freedom of the American settlers in Texas.

> *The Texas Revolution came in 1836*
> *at the Alamo where Texans nobly died.*
> *But their struggles were avenged on the San Jacinto plains*
> *where the fledgling Texas Army turned the tide.*

The Texans had been content to be citizens of Mexico. But when their freedom was taken away and the Mexican government tried to move many of them out of Texas, they could not tolerate that treatment. They then organized the Texas Revolution.

The Texans signed their **Declaration of Independence** on March 2, 1836. This occurred while the **Battle of the Alamo** was actually in progress. Santa Ana wanted to put down the revolution and expel the Americans from Texas. He won the famous battles at the Alamo in San Antonio and at Goliad in 1835, but was finally defeated by the Texas Army at a place called **San Jacinto**, near present day Houston. In fact, the city of Houston was named after **General Sam Houston**, the victorious commander of the Texas Army.

> *The importance of this battle, do not underestimate. The impact*
> *of the conflict must be known.*
> *For it meant that all or portions of the western states,*
> *th' United States would ultimately own.*

In world history, few battles have had more impact than the battles of the Texas Revolution. These were very small battles by all standards of warfare, even in those days. The Texas Army had only a few hundred men. And they defeated a Mexican army with numbers estimated at up to 6,000. When you consider the contributions made to the United States from the great Western states, you must remember that had it not been for the Texas Revolution, this entire region might still be a part of Mexico.

Texas was actually an independent nation for almost ten years. The people had wanted to join the United States from the very beginning, but there were problems which prevented this from happening. The Northern states did not want to admit another slave state. Also, the great powers of Europe, including England and France, did not want Texas to join the Union. They feared the United States would become too powerful if they took control of that entire region. During this time, when Texas was a republic, settlers came from many countries of Europe and established themselves in towns and regions of the territory.

> *When Texas joined the Union back in 1845,*
> *a new conflict with Mexico began.*
> *Mexico did claim much of Texas property,*
> *and said the border was not the Rio Grande.*
>
> *War was declared back in 1846,*
> *and the battles did continue two long years.*
> *In the treaty, on the map, California and Utah,*
> *Arizona and Nevada did appear.*

After the Battle of San Jacinto when Texas became an independent republic, there was never an established peace with Mexico. A treaty was never signed where Mexico recognized or accepted the fact that Texas should be treated as an independent nation.

When Texas was accepted into the United States, however, this created a new problem for Mexico. Now the Mexican government had to deal with the government of the United States regarding the official borders of Texas. A war between the United States and Mexico started in 1846. The battles continued over a two-year period. Of course, the United States was much more powerful and won the war very easily. A treaty of peace, **The Treaty of Guadalupe Hidalgo,** was signed in 1848 in which Mexico recognized the Rio Grande as the boundary between Texas and Mexico. Other boundaries in the areas farther west were also agreed upon. In return, the United States paid Mexico $15 million for the land.

> *With the Gadsden Purchase in 1853,*
> *the southern border took its final shape.*
> *We bought that strip of land so a railroad one day might be able to*
> *cross the southern states.*

The current border between Mexico and the United States was not complete after that treaty in 1848, however. Just five years later, the United States bought another narrow strip of land from Mexico, in the southern part of what is now Arizona and New Mexico. This was called the **Gadsden Purchase.** They bought the land so that another transcontinental railroad line could be built across the southern states. Without that section of land, it would have been much more difficult to build the railroad through those western mountains.

> *The northwest lands in those early Western days*
> *were by England and the U.S. jointly shared.*
> *But after settlers headed West on the Oregon Trail,*
> *a negotiated border was prepared.*

After it became clear that the lands of Texas and the Southwest would become part of the United States, there was only one large region that was not yet part of the United States. That was the **Oregon Territory.** Traveling to the Oregon Territory was not easy. The Oregon Trail was 2,000 miles long. Settlers had to cross two ranges of high and dangerous mountains. That was most difficult in covered wagons pulled by horses or oxen across the rough trails of those days. The settlers also had to defend themselves from attacks by Indians. It took brave and hearty souls to make such a journey.

The Oregon Territory was a beautiful and fertile land. As good news about the territory spread to the states of the East, thousands of settlers joined great wagon trains to the new land.

Prior to this time, the territory was owned jointly by England and the United States. Since very few white men actually lived there, it didn't really matter which country officially owned it. However, as more and more Americans poured into the land, both England and the United States realized that a boundary would have to be drawn.

The Oregon Territory at that time included the present states of Oregon, Washington, Idaho and parts of Wyoming and Montana, as well as the present-day province of British Columbia in Canada. In 1846, England and the United States agreed upon the current boundary that separates the United States and Canada.

With that agreement, the United States achieved its present size and boundaries as it relates to the 48 states that join each other. About 100 years later, two more states, Alaska and Hawaii would join the Union.

> That, my friend, tells the story how the West was won
> in the eighteenth and the nineteenth centuries.
> How Americans conquered this great expanse
> and established it from sea to shining sea.

This expansion of the nation occurred over a period of 63 years from the signing of the Treaty of Paris in 1782 to the signing of the agreement establishing the borders for the Oregon Territory in 1846.

This was a difficult process. Most of the territory was acquired by negotiation, and some of it was acquired by war. Another struggle took place during this process. That was the struggle between the Indians and the white settlers who were taking control of the land.

The settling of the new land was not an easy process. There were no roads. Food and water were often in short supply. Men had to cross mountains and deserts. They had to fight diseases. They had conflicts with the Indians. It required people with an optimistic and fighting spirit, people who desired opportunity and who were willing to pay the price. That is the kind of people who founded America. That is the kind of people who built America, and made it the great nation that it is today.

Study Questions:

1. If you had been a young person living in the eastern states, living a safe and comfortable life, what would make you want to go west?

2. Do you think the white men had any right to go and settle in the western lands which were occupied by the Indians?

3. If you had been a person intent on going to the west, how would you have worked with the Indians?

4. Why was the Mississippi River such an important waterway for the Americans?

5. If you had been advising Napoleon as to whether or not he should sell the Louisiana Territory to the United States, what would you have told him? How would you have advised him? To sell or not to sell?

6. The leaders of the United States felt it was important for them to own all the land from the Atlantic to the Pacific within the northern and southern borders. List several reasons why you think they felt this way.

7. Why was it important that Texas be admitted into the Union? How could the United States have been hurt if Texas had remained an independent republic?

8. Why was it important that the Oregon Territory be admitted to the Union?

The Transcontinental Railroad

About the music...
(Tape 2, Song 4)

The music for this song is done in a country music style called "bluegrass." The predominant instruments are the guitar, the banjo, and the bass fiddle. The cheerful sound of an old-fashioned railroad whistle is added to give the flavor of the railroad. It is played in a cheerful, major key to a lilting bluegrass rhythm. If you listen closely you can hear the "ch ch ch ch" sound of the steam locomotive wheels played by a percussion instrument called "the high hat."

Oh, once this nation was an untamed land
    East and West were divided by a mighty span,
Full of mountains and prairies where the wild wind blows,
    Then the country started growin' where the railroad goes.

Chorus

Where the railroad goes, where the railroad goes;
    America is growin' where the railroad goes.

They struck gold in California in 1849;
    Men rushed to the West to seek their fortunes in the mines.
But they had to go through Panama or clear around Cape Horn
    Or they scaled the mighty mountains and the deserts full of thorns.

Chorus

Well, their journey was a long one full of terrible travails.
    Some died in stormy shipwrecks or on steamy jungle trails.
The ones who crossed the country in those wild West days
    Faced heat and cold and suffering, even Indian raids.

Chorus

In '61, the Civil War had only just begun;
    California was a new state and a prize to be won;
The Pacific Railroad Act was passed in order to ensure
    California's Union loyalty would certainly endure.

Chorus

Back west in California, the wealth increased.
    They opened trade with China and the great Far East.
They grew crops and dug min'rals, copper, ores, and gold
    But they needed iron rails so the goods could be sold.

Chorus

The planning for the project was the greatest of its time;
    Locomotives from New York, iron rails from eastern mines;
To ship around the continents took more than half a year
    Before they could arrive on San Francisco's pier.

Chorus

The Central Pacific started from the west;
    Began in Sacramento, faced a tough and mighty test;
The Union Pacific was their rival in the east;
    From Omaha, they laid the rails, the labor never ceased.

Chorus

The obstacles they faced were far too great to be ignored,
    To cross the rugged mountains and the mighty rivers ford.
They built across the deserts and the prairies of the plains,
    Fought heat and cold and Indians o'er the vast terrains.

Chorus

They chipped out mountain tunnels and fought the burning heat.
    Iron men against exposure, even buffalo stampedes.
There were farmers, miners, convicts, crooked gamblers and more,
    And veterans from North and South who'd fought the Civil War.

Chorus

The corruption with the money was a story to be told.
    Robber baron crooks lined their pockets full of gold.
There were Senators and Congressmen impeached and vilified,
    But that didn't stop the railroad as it crossed the Great Divide.

Chorus

In the West, the railroad workers deserted to the mines
    So they hired Chinese laborers who got there just in time.
From the East, they hired Irishmen, who'd traveled to the states,
    To seek out wealth and fortune to improve their low estates.

Chorus

For the Indians, the railroad was a tragedy at hand.
    The white man crossed their hunting grounds and drove them from their land.
They knew their ancient way of life was coming to a close,
    For progress caused injustice and uncounted human woes.

Chorus

Alongside railroad work camps sprung up little Western towns.
    Drunken swindlers and con men, and gamblers all around.
They took the workers' money with their schemes and crooked deals.
    That's why those little shanty towns were called "hell on wheels."

Chorus

After seven years of toil and sweat, through blist'ring heat and cold,
    At Promontory, Utah, they drove that spike of gold.
The people of America were feelin' oh, so fine;
    They'd accomplished the impossible in 1869.

Chorus

The Transcontinental Railroad

"What was it the engine said?
Pilots touching—head to head
Facing on a single track
Half a world behind each back."

-Brett Harte, a poem describing the two engines facing each other at the dedication of the Transcontinental Railroad, May 10, 1869

"Drill, my Paddy's, drill
Drill all day, no sugar in your tay,
Working on the U.P. Rail Road.
And drill! and blast! and fire!
Drill, my heroes, drill."

-A popular song sung by the workers during the building of the great railroad.

Oh, once this nation was an untamed land
East and West were divided by a mighty span,
Full of mountains and prairies where the wild wind blows,
Then the country started growin' where the railroad goes.

Chorus

Where the railroad goes, where the railroad goes;
America is growin' where the railroad goes.

The men who discovered America had no idea how big this country really was. In fact, when the King of England granted charters to people, he sometime specified the northern and southern boundaries and granted them all the land to the West clear to the Pacific Ocean. Before the Constitution was ratified by the states, new boundaries for the states were agreed upon.

The United States is 3,000 miles across from East to West. In those days before modern transportation, it took about half a year just to cross the country.

The invention of the railroad totally changed the way people traveled. The first trains were pulled by horses. Then, with the invention of the steam engine in the early 1800's, modern trains came into being. The first railroad in America was built in about 1830. Those early railroad lines connected the great cities of the East. The idea of a railroad to the West was not practical before the 1850's. There were very few people in the West, not enough to justify the building of something so expensive as a railroad. Also, few people ever went west of the Mississippi River.

From the very beginning, one of the objectives of those who explored America was to find a water route to the Pacific Ocean so they could more easily trade with China. Expeditions to the West soon revealed the vastness of the North American Continent.

> *They struck gold in California in 1849;*
> *Men rushed to the West to seek their fortunes in the mines.*
> *But they had to go through Panama or clear around Cape Horn*
> *Or they scaled the mighty mountains and the deserts full of thorns.*

In 1849, gold was found in Sutter's estate in California. His efforts to keep the secret quickly failed. Very soon, fortune seekers swarmed to California to "get rich quick." But if a man wanted to go to California, he had only three choices: 1) he could go by ship all the way around South America, 2) he could travel by ship down the Atlantic coast to Panama, cross the jungles of Panama to the Pacific coast, then catch another ship up to San Francisco, or 3) he could travel by land across the West.

> *Well, their journey was a long one full of terrible travails.*
> *Some died in stormy shipwrecks or on steamy jungle trails.*
> *The ones who crossed the country in those wild West days*
> *Faced heat and cold and suffering, even Indian raids.*

The tip of South America is called **Cape Horn**. That area has always been known for its rough storms. Many ships sank in those stormy waters, and many a passenger lost his life on that dangerous journey.

The journey through Panama was also dangerous. A person saved some time not having to sail around South America, but the Central American jungles had disease-carrying mosquitoes. Many people died of tropical diseases on that journey. In fact, the most enthusiastic promoter of the railroad, **Theodore Judah**, died of a tropical disease after one of his trips through Panama.

Those who traveled across the West also faced hardships. There were high mountains, dry, hot deserts, and endless stretches of plains. There was also the threat of raids by hostile Indians. Regardless of the way a person traveled, the trip was hard and dangerous.

> *In '61, the Civil War had only just begun;*
> *California was a new state and a prize to be won;*
> *The Pacific Railroad Act was passed in order to ensure*
> *California's Union loyalty would certainly endure.*

When the southern states left the Union before the Civil War and formed the Confederate States of America, both the Union and the Confederacy wanted California to join them. The northern states knew that if they could build a railroad to California, that state would certainly become a part of the Union where they could trade freely over the railroad line. For that reason, Congress passed a law called **The Pacific Railroad Act** and provided money for the building of the railroad.

Back west in California, the wealth increased.
They opened trade with China and the great Far East.
They grew crops and dug min'rals, copper, ores, and gold
But they needed iron rails so the goods could be sold.

When the thousands of treasure seekers reached the West Coast, most did not strike it rich with gold. But they did find rich farm land and other natural resources. They settled in the land and started new lives there. Now there was a need for a safe, fast means of travel to the East. There were a few men who dreamed of building a railroad, but most people thought this would be impossible. Those men were considered to be fanatics. One of those men was named Theodore Judah. They gave him the nickname, "Crazy Judah."

The planning for the project was the greatest of its time;
Locomotives from New York, iron rails from eastern mines;
To ship around the continents took more than half a year
Before they could arrive on San Francisco's pier.

Can you imagine the problems of planning to build a railroad across America? How would they ship thousands of tons of iron rails from the mines and factories of the East to the building sites in the West? How would they ship steam locomotives and rail cars to California? Just think of the cost of such an endeavor. It was the greatest and most expensive project ever undertaken in America up to that time.

The Central Pacific started from the west;
Began in Sacramento, faced a tough and mighty test;
The Union Pacific was their rival in the east;
From Omaha, they laid the rails, the labor never ceased.

Congress selected two railroad companies to build the railroad. The one that started in California with the task of building toward the East was the **Central Pacific Railroad**. In the east, railroads already existed and went as far west as Omaha, Nebraska. A railroad company called the **Union Pacific** was selected to start at Omaha and build toward the West.

Early Railroad

The obstacles they faced were far too great to be ignored,
To cross the rugged mountains and the mighty rivers ford.
They built across the deserts and the prairies of the plains,
Fought heat and cold and Indians o'er the vast terrains.

They chipped out mountain tunnels and fought the burning heat.
Iron men against exposure, even buffalo stampedes.
They were farmers, miners, convicts, crooked gamblers and more,
And veterans from North and South who'd fought the Civil War.

This was no small project for either company. They had to design and build great bridges across rivers and lowlands. The working conditions for the workers were hard. The biggest problem of all was a steep mountain range in California called the **Sierra Nevada**. It took brave and tough men to do a job like this.

The corruption with the money was a story to be told.
Robber baron crooks lined their pockets full of gold.
There were Senators and Congressmen impeached and vilified,
but that didn't stop the railroad as it crossed the Great Divide.

During the nineteenth century, America began to change from an **agrarian society** to an **industrialized society**. (An agrarian society is one in which most people live in the country or small towns and make their living through farming and agriculture. In an industrialized society, more people make a living working in manufacturing jobs.) The building of factories required a great deal of money. Bankers became wealthy loaning money to people who built great factories and industries. Whenever there is a lot of money around, there are always dishonest people who want to find a way to put some of the money into their own pockets through dishonest means. In those days, such men were called **robber barons**.

Robber barons were businessmen who took unfair advantage of people in order to make themselves rich. Since that time, Congress has had to pass laws to prevent people from doing those kinds of business activities.

The Transcontinental Railroad was one of the most expensive projects in the history of the United States. Just think of the cost of buying the materials and the equipment used to build the railroad and the cost of paying all the workers. The money was supplied by the federal government and by people who bought shares of stock in the railroad companies. Many of the men who owned the railroad companies found ways to divert some of the money into their own pockets. These were not the kind of criminals who use guns to do their evil deeds. These were respectable-looking men who looked honest on the outside but were dishonest on the inside. Some of these men were even members of Congress.

In the West, the railroad workers deserted to the mines
So they hired Chinese laborers who got there just in time.
From the East, they hired Irishmen, who'd traveled to the states,
To seek out wealth and fortune and improve their low estates.

Railroad construction was hard work. Where did they find men like this? They came from all walks of life. When the Civil War ended, many men had lost everything. The railroad offered them a good job. In California, many of the workers signed on with the railroad with no intention of doing any work. They simply wanted a free ride to other parts of the West. At one point, there were rumors of rich minerals in Nevada. The tales of prospectors quickly reached the ears of money-hungry adventurers in California. Men hired on with the railroad, went as far as Nevada, then took the railroad's tools and deserted to work in the mines, where they could make more money. This became a serious problem. Then the railroad managers came up with a brilliant idea. They hired workers from China. They offered them free passage from China and a chance to live in America. The workers, who were called "Coolies," labored very hard. They proved to be more reliable than the American workers.

When they were building through the mountains, they had to use picks and shovels to dig their way. It took years to accomplish this monumental task. Many workers lost their footing and fell off mountain ledges to their deaths.

For the Indians, the railroad was a tragedy at hand.
The white man crossed their hunting grounds and drove them from their land.
They knew their ancient way of life was coming to a close,
For progress caused injustice and uncounted human woes.

The Transcontinental Railroad was not good news for everyone. For the original Americans, the Indians, it was very bad news, indeed. The Indians had lost much of their land when the white man began moving to the West. But for many years, the states west of the Mississippi River were still untouched by the white man. Indians could still roam the plains living off of the buffalo the way their forefathers had done for many centuries.

With the coming of the railroad, people began to establish ranches, farms, and towns in the Western territories. Of course, these were built on lands that had always belonged to the Indians. Some men paid for the land, but many did not.

The Indians knew what had happened to other tribes in the East, and they did not want to lose their land or their way of life. To try to stop the white men who were building the railroad, the Indians fought, but the white men brought armies to fight back. The Indians knew their way of life was coming to an end. How sad it is that this could not have been done in a more just way. Some Indian tribes got along with the white men, but others did not. Many people lost their lives in the struggles and battles that occurred when the West was being taken over by the white man.

> *Alongside railroad work camps sprung up little Wild West towns.*
> *Drunken swindlers and con men, and gamblers all around.*
> *They took the workers' money with their schemes and crooked deals.*
> *That's why those little shanty towns were called "hell on wheels."*

The men who worked on the railroad were rough men, men who did heavy manual labor from early in the morning until the sun went down at night. Because the railroad building moved forward each day, the workers had to move down the line as the roadbeds, tracks and trestles were completed. They lived in tents and wagons. They were almost always unmarried men or men whose families lived in cities far away. These men entertained themselves in bar rooms. To provide this type of entertainment, there were others who built little towns near the work camps. Still others had wagons and large tents that moved along with the portable railroad work camps.

The railroad workers would go to these little shanty towns on the weekends and get very drunk. Many of the workers thought they could get rich quickly by gambling. There was no shortage of dishonest gamblers, bar keepers, and lying businessmen who took advantage of the workers. Many times a man would come into town on Saturday with his paycheck from the railroad and lose it all over the drunken, rowdy weekend. He would return to the work camp with not a penny in his pocket.

> *After seven years of toil and sweat, through blist'ring heat and cold,*
> *At Promontory, Utah, they drove that spike of gold.*
> *The people of America were feelin' oh, so fine;*
> *They'd accomplished the impossible in 1869.*

Construction on the Transcontinental Railroad started in 1863 in California and in 1865 in Omaha. The Union Pacific had to build their lines across a range of the Rocky Mountains called **"The Great Divide,"** and the Central Pacific, building from California, had to cross another very steep range called the **Sierra Nevada**.

The two railroad companies competed with each other to build the most miles of track. The federal government paid them based on the number of miles of track they laid. So, whichever company laid the most track earned the most money.

As the two companies labored on month after month from two different directions, the meeting place was established in a place called Promontory, Utah. A great ceremony was planned to mark the completion of the railroad. During the ceremony, they were to drive the final spike of the entire project. The spike was made of solid gold. Government officials and dignitaries came from all over the nation. Newspapers and telegraph companies covered this great event. All of America cheered when the telegraph companies reported that the golden spike had been hammered into that last wooden crosstie.

The Transcontinental Railroad changed America. It brought the East and the West together. It made it possible for goods shipped to California from China and the Far East to be transferred quickly and inexpensively to the eastern states. It opened up the West to pioneer families who wanted to establish farms and ranches in the West. It made possible the mining of valuable minerals in the western states which otherwise could not have been transported to the East and the rest of the world. In a sense, it fulfilled the work of the King of England way back in 1607 when he desired to find a passage across America to India.

By the end of the 1800's, there would be five transcontinental railroad lines which would cross America. But it was that first monumental victory of completing the line from Sacramento, California, to Omaha, Nebraska, which proved to the people of America, and the world, that great things could be accomplished in America.

Study Questions:

1. It seems that all of the Congressmen and Senators would have been in favor of a transcontinental railroad in the 1800s, yet many thought it was a foolish venture. Why do you think they felt that way?

2. If you had been a Congressman in favor of building the Transcontinental Railroad, how would you have argued in favor of the project? That is, what would you have said to those who opposed it?

3. If you had been appointed by the president to be in charge of making peace with the Indians, how would you have made the railroad project a fair deal for the Indians?

4. What were the major benefits of the Transcontinental Railroad to this country?

5. The Transcontinental Railroad was the largest and most expensive project ever undertaken by the United States in that day. What are some other major projects this country has undertaken and accomplished?

Golden Spike

Appendix

The study questions do not necessarily have any one right or wrong answer. There is no "answer key" which gives an expected answer. The idea is for the students to go through the thought processes, evaluate the issues from each point of view, and come up with the answer that seems right to them.

How to Use this Program

There are many creative ways in which this program can be used to transfer the great ideas of history to our children's minds. This section will give you some basic ideas showing how to use it for individual or class instruction.

Step One: Listen to the Song

Listen to the song. The main objective of the first hearing of the song is simply to become accustomed to the tune and the structure. Since there are many verses and repetitions, it should be easy to learn the tune after one complete repetition of the song.

For example, listen to the first song, "Roanoke and Jamestown." You will notice it follows a pattern of two verses followed by a chorus. The chorus repeats after every two verses.

Step Two: Read and Listen to the Song

Read the words of the song silently as you listen. It would be best to do this two times, as the repetition will enhance the learning of the facts.

Step Three: Read the Book

The section in the book that corresponds to the song is designed to be a commentary or explanation of each verse of the song. Because of the nature of the poetry in the songs, some of the words may be new to the students. Any new or difficult words will be explained in the story section immediately following the verse. Important words will be noted in bold print. These are the names of people, places, things, concepts and ideas which will amplify the material in the songs. The words of the song will generally provide all of the common knowledge anyone would need to know about the subject material.

The general idea is not to require students to memorize all of the details. If the students will simply learn the songs, they should know enough general information to be conversant about the subject.

For example, in "Roanoke and Jamestown," the song says,

> The English governor returned to take his place,
> but found that the settlers disappeared without a trace.

The story in the book amplifies this and tells how the settlers carved the word "Croatoan" on a certain tree to leave a message as to their whereabouts. While this may be interesting information, it goes beyond that which the students would actually need to know about the subject of Jamestown.

Step Four: Sing Along With the Tape/CD

Sing along with the tape/CD which has both the voice and the music. The words will soon become second nature.

Step Five: Sing Along with the Music Only

The try singing along with the sound track without the voice. This will cement the song into the minds of the students.

Step Six: Discuss the Study Questions

The study questions are designed to promote higher-level thinking on the subject covered by each song. These questions do not simply ask for a "regurgitation" of memorized facts. They require the students to utilize and analyze the information they have learned and grapple with the same kinds of issues which our forefathers faced. This is one of the major purposes for the study of history because we must eventually deal with the same ideas in our world today and tomorrow.

Optional Projects

For a class, divide the song into parts and have individual students or small groups memorize one or more verses. Then go through the entire song having each individual or small group sing their part.

An alternative to singing would be the "readers' theater." Small groups of students would be assigned sections of the poem to read in a chorus fashion. This is also a very effective way to improve students' reading skills.

Have each individual or group explain the verse or verses which they have memorized to the entire group.

Have the students investigate the types of clothing worn during the period of history. If resources permit, have them make costumes.

Ballads of American History Song Book

Table Of Contents

A Declaration by the Representatives of the UNITED STATES OF AMERICA, in General Congress assembled.

When in the course of human events it becomes necessary for one people to dissolve the political bands which have connected them with another, and to assume among the powers of the earth the separate and equal station to which the laws of nature & of nature's god entitle them, a decent respect to the opinions of mankind requires that they should declare the causes which impel them to the separation.

We hold these truths to be self-evident; that all men are created equal, that they are endowed by their creator with inherent & inalienable rights; that among these are life, & liberty, & the pursuit of happiness; that to secure these ends, governments are instituted among men, deriving their just powers from the consent of the governed; that whenever any form of government becomes destructive of these ends, it is the right of the people to alter or to abolish it, & to institute new government, laying it's foundation on such principles & organising it's powers in such form, as to them shall seem most likely to effect their safety & happiness. prudence indeed will dictate that governments long established should not be changed for light & transient causes: and accordingly all experience hath shewn that mankind are more disposed to suffer while evils are sufferable, than to right themselves by abolishing the forms to which they are accustomed. but when a long train of abuses & usurpations [begun at a distinguished period & pursuing invariably the same object, evinces a design to reduce them under absolute Despotism,] it is their right, it is their duty, to throw off such & to provide new guards for their future security. such has been the patient sufferance of these colonies; & such is now the necessity which constrains them to expunge their former systems of government. the history of the present king of Great Britain is a history of unremitting injuries and usurpations, among which appears no solitary fact to contradict the uniform tenor of the rest but all have in direct object the establishment of an absolute tyranny over these states. to prove this, let facts be submitted to a candid world for the truth of which we pledge a faith yet unsullied by falsehood.

Queen Elizabeth sought for English pride.
  She wanted for her country a colony to guide.
They knew about the New World in that land across the sea.
  That land we call America, uncivilized but free.

Sir Walter Raleigh planned that colony abroad.
  The Queen gave him a charter to rule that foreign sod.
He hired two sea captains who Roanoke Island claimed;
  In honor of their good Queen, Virginia, it was named.

Chorus

They came from England, across the stormy sea.
  They came to found a new land for you and me.

In 1585, they took one hundred men,
  To found on Roanoke Island the colony for them.
The men sought gold and fortune rather than to tame the land.
  But the project failed and they returned to England once again.

Two years later, Sir Walter tried once more.
  He sent a group of families to settle this new shore.
To found such a colony was dangerous indeed.
  These people had commitment, a tough and noble breed.

Chorus

Back to England went the governor; because he realized,
  Their project soon would fail unless they had some new supplies.
But England was involved in a great sea war with Spain.
  For three long years, in England did the governor remain.

The English governor returned to take his place.
  But found that the settlers disappeared without a trace.
They sent several ships who did seek and search in vain.
  But the lost Roanoke colony was never found again.

The Virginia Colonies

Chorus

Twenty long years later, King James was on the throne,
 He thought once more the New World was for Englishmen to own.
There was a group of merchants called the London Company,
 Who hired ships and men to once more cross the stormy sea.

The King sought for a passage to India by sea.
 He hoped for gold and riches to flow continuously.
To find the Lost Colony of Roanoke was their hope.
 Also, to spread the gospel to all the native folk.

Chorus

In choosing new colonists to make the trip succeed,
 Half were wealthy gentlemen who'd never worked indeed.
They thought that gold and fortune soon would quickly come their way.
 Then they'd return to England far richer men one day.

In Sixteen Seven, they came in vessels three.
 They entered the James River to found their colony.
They chose their land unwisely near a swamp where varmints thrive.
 Mosquitoes and diseases took their toll of human lives.

Chorus

Captain John Smith was the man who took control.
 He forced the Jamestown colonists, each man to pull his load.
When one day he was injured, to England he returned.
 Starvation took its toll when idle men their work did spurn.

Of those five hundred men who tried to make the project thrive.
 Only sixty souls the hardships did survive.
As they started back to England, they were greeted by new men.
 So, they returned and settled little Jamestown once again.

Chorus

They began their work again under leadership anew.
Slowly, through hard work a new success they did pursue.
When, in 1619, ninety women did arrive,
They married Englishmen and with families they did thrive.

Tobacco was the crop which brought the pay they long had sought.
They finally realized their search for gold was all for naught.
But the greatest wealth of Jamestown in that World across the sea,
Was the chance to build a life in a land that would be free.

Chorus

The Plymouth Colony

Words by Fred Cooper
Music by Diane Solo

In 1600, King James did reign.
    He ruled all England and its vast domain.
The Church of England did the King sustain,
    But other churches did he thus restrain.

Many people in that day did try,
    The Church of England, then, to purify.
The state religion did not satisfy.
    Their faith in God they would not deny.

Chorus

The Pilgrims suffered in those early years.
    Their faith sustained them through their toil and tears.

King James resisted with a heavy hand.
    Imprisoned Puritans throughout the land.
The persecution did their faith expand.
    Their dedication was a thing so grand.

The King's fierce anger they could not ignore.
    They fled for safety o'er to Holland's shore.
Religious freedom did they find in store,
    But with Dutch culture they had no rapport.

Chorus

The New World was a place where they could go.
    Where seeds of faith and life could freely grow.
The King, a charter he did then bestow.
    The winds of freedom, then, would surely blow.

These hardy Pilgrims did one day set sail.
    One hundred Englishmen who would not fail.
Their six week journey filled with great travail,
    Through many hardships would they then prevail.

The Plymouth Colony

Chorus

To sail to Jamestown was their first intent,
    but stormy weather just would not relent.
So far from Virginia, the Mayflower went
    to northern reaches of the continent.

In 1620 did the Lord provide,
    off Plymouth's shore the Pilgrims did arrive.
They set a village in the countryside,
    just four short days before the Christmastide.

Chorus

The land was north of England's sure domain.
    There were no rulers on this new terrain.
The Mayflower Compact did their law contain;
    So law and order in the land would reign,

That first long winter there were hardships great.
    The food supply could not accommodate.
Disease did half their numbers decimate;
    Their courage, one could never overstate.

Chorus

In Springtime, Samoset and Squanto came;
    They taught them how to farm and capture game;
The Indians their lasting friends became.
    A friendship covenant did the men proclaim.

The Autumn brought abundant harvesting;
    To God their words of praise and thanks did ring.
The Indians joined this happy gathering.
    They shared a feast we now call Thanksgiving.

Chorus

Somoset Visits Plymouth

The Thirteen Colonies

Words & Music by Fred Cooper

Just after 1600, to America there came,
    courageous folk from Europe whose spirits were aflame.
Some came to worship freely, others sought for fortunes grand.
    But all sought for a new life in this large and untamed land.

Virginia was the first one; by Englishmen 'twas formed.
    These men had heard that gold and fortune lay for them in store.
They came in 1607; many men did not survive.
    Tobacco brought the wealth that gold and silver had denied.

Chorus

The colonies were formed by both the humble and the great.
    And from these thirteen colonies, they formed the United States.

The colony of Georgia was first claimed by France and Spain.
    In 1629, a group of English merchants came.
In 17 and 30, it was named for good King George.
    'Twas prisoners and debtors, the first lasting township forged.

In the 1500's was South Carolina claimed,
    by unsuccessful settlers from the land of Spain.
King Charles of old England in 1633,
    did grant the land to Englishmen who settled there indeed.

Chorus

North Carolina's early story was the same.
    In 17 and 12, the land got its new name.
German and Swiss settlers were the first ones in the land,
    but King Charles of Great Britain did later take command.

The Swedish and the Dutch men first settled Delaware.
    But the English won New Netherlands to Holland's great despair.
It soon became a part of Pennsylvania, and then,
    in 1704, it separated once again.

Chorus

Maryland was for the Virgin Mary surely named.
　　For Roman Catholic settlers, church freedom was obtained,
But much religious fighting continued through the years.
　　The king appointed governors, the colony to steer.

New Jersey was discovered back in 1524.
　　One hundred years thereafter, Swedes and Dutch men came ashore.
The Englishmen then conquered Dutch possessions in the land.
　　Religious freedom reigned when Quaker owners took their stand.

Chorus

The French and the Dutch both occupied New York,
　　But English armies took control in 1664.
The Dutch and English trappers with the Indians did trade,
　　But French and English wars, the white men's settlement delayed.

The Puritans and Pilgrims settled Massachusetts' shores.
　　They sought religious freedom from their British overlords.
They were friendly with the Indians who helped them to survive.
　　But over foreign politics with the English they did strive.

Chorus

The settlers of Connecticut from Massachusetts came.
　　Founded small religious colonies in their churches' names.
They wanted independence from the King of England's laws.
　　They were among the first to speak their mind in freedom's cause.

Those who formed Rhode Island came from Massachusetts, too;
　　To practice their religion without government adieu.
The land was rich and fertile, their ports were hubs of trade.
　　Independent church and state foundations there were laid.

The Thirteen Colonies

Chorus

New Hampshire was established by decision of King James.
　　Two English noblemen were given major land domains.
At first, it was a part of Massachusetts colony.
　　The king, the land divided so they'd function separately.

King James gave a charter to a man named, William Penn,
　　A land once owned by Sweden and the Netherlands.
The Quakers for religious freedom ventured to this land.
　　They were first to place the government in the people's hands.

Chorus

These colonies, at first, behaved like independent states.
　　But all were ruled by England through the monarch's designates.
Some were loyal to the king, while others soon rebelled.
　　One day they got together; a new nation they beheld.

Chorus

The Revolutionary War

Words & Music by Fred Cooper

In sev-en-teen six-ty three, the Bri-tish had vic-to-ry. They won the French and In-dian War their strength was plain to see. They owned the land of Can-a-da and all the A-mer-i-can South from the coast of No-va Sco-tia to the Miss-is-sip-pi's mouth. Get rea-dy me boys, now call to arms, now what are ye wait-in' for, the A-mer-i-cans got to win the Rev-o-lu-tion-ar-y War.

In 1763, the British had victory.
   They won the French and Indian War. Their strength was plain to see.
They owned the land of Canada and all the American South.
   From the coast of Nova Scotia to the Mississippi's mouth.

Chorus

Get ready, me boys and call to arms, so what are ye waitin' for;
   The Americans got to win the Revolutionary War.

The English had the colonies under their control;
   There were thirteen separate governments to do as the King extolled.
They reasoned the Americans should pay the English crown,
   for the British troops defended all their villages and towns.

Parliament made the laws that ruled the colonists' fate.
   But colonial representatives could not participate.
They told where they could sail their ships and sell their goods in trade,
   and made them pay stiff taxes on the things that England made.

Chorus

In 1773, the people's remedy was to boycott English
   products like sugar, coffee and tea.
The merchants back in England began to feel a loss.
   They petitioned to the Parliament to cut the taxes' cost.

Still acting stubbornly, the British taxed the tea.
   Bostonians dumped a cargo load one night into the sea.
The Boston Tea Party brought anger to the King.
   He blockaded Boston Harbor with the goods the ships could bring.

Chorus

In 1774, freedom was the cause.
   The Continental Congress formed to protest British laws.
They told the folks to arm themselves in case of a British attack.
   The colonists would defend themselves and strike the Redcoats back.

In 1775, the battle flag unfurled,
  from Lexington and Concord came "the shot heard round the world."
Paul Revere shouted the warning. The Minutemen came out.
  They drove the Brits to Boston town and showed they had some clout.

Chorus

At the Battle of Bunker Hill, the bloodiest day of the War,
  the British drove the colonists from the hill they were fightin' for.
Then, the colonists formed an army, a rough and tumble band,
  who fought the Redcoats bravely for the conquest of the land.

The Continental Congress met again in '75;
  Formed the Continental Army to keep the fight alive.
They retook the town of Boston and drove the British out,
  but the war was just beginnin' and the outcome was in doubt.

Chorus

They fought the war in Canada and in Southern colonies.
  But in '75, the British seemed to have the victory.
Some Americans still were loyal to the British crown.
  They even joined the redcoats, the uprising to put down.

In 1776, the Congress met again;
  Declared their independence from the British ruler.
Then, they wrote a Declaration to tell the world just why.
  Their right to split from England was most surely justified.

Chorus

It said that from the people came the right of governing;
  That the laws of nature and nature's God were greater than the King.
It listed the abuses of the British crown,
  and declared the thirteen colonies were independent now.

Philadelphia was captured one year later by King George.
　　Americans spent the winter months in the town of Valley Forge.
They suffered many hardships, and many of them died;
　　But noble General Washington, on God he still relied.

Chorus

The colonies needed allies to help with supplies and men.
　　They called on England's rivals, the nations of France and Spain.
Vic'try at Saratoga proved the Yanks could win.
　　So the allies sent the ships and guns to help the war to end.

In the western lands, the British troops with Indians allied;
　　To try to force the patriots from the countryside.
In Illinois and Indiana, American troops did reign,
　　to oust the British army from the claim to western plains.

Chorus

In '78, the southern states entered in the war.
　　To Georgia and Carolina marched the British army corps.
In two long years, the patriots in the countryside did fight,
　　to take the land that England won. They fought with all their might.

In 1781, to Yorktown they did run.
　　The French had sent their Navy just to help the Americans.
They surrounded British forces on both the land and sea,
　　'till Cornwallis did surrender, and the colonies were free.

Chorus

In 1783, at long last they did sign,
　　The Treaty of Paris at the Palace of Versailles.
After seven years of fighting, they had their victory.
　　The United States of America, a nation now could be.

Chorus

The Constitution

Words & Music by Fred Cooper

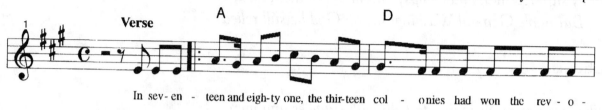

In sev- en - teen and eigh-ty one, the thir-teen col - onies had won the rev-o-

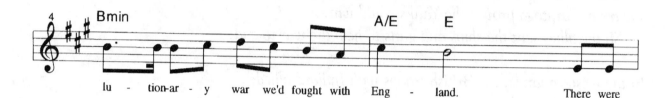

lu - tion-ar - y war we'd fought with Eng - land. There were

thir - teen sep - 'rate states re - luc - tant to co - o - per - ate and form a

un - ion in this new land. The found - ing

fa - thers' last - ing con - tri - bu - tion was the Con - sti -

tu - tion of th'U - ni - ted States

In 17 and 81, the 13 colonies had won
    the Revolutionary War we'd fought with England.
There were 13 sep'rate states reluctant to cooperate
    and form a union in this new land.

Chorus

The founding fathers' lasting contribution
    was the Constitution of the United States

The very year the war o'er, they signed new governing accords
    The Articles of Confederation.
They guaranteed autonomy and independent sovereignty
    to each dominion in this new land.

Chorus

But this new government was weak, outlook for compromise was bleak
    they had no authority to levy taxes.
All thirteen states had to agree to then accomplish anything
    they did together in this new land.

Chorus

In Philadelphia was held a meeting quite unparalleled
    which they called the Constitutional Convention.
They wrote a document so strong, it would establish right and wrong
    for that great nation in this new land.

Chorus

A new republic was conceived. No man could ever then receive
    full power over this entire nation.
The people had the right to rule, responsibility to choose
    the ones to govern in this new land.

Chorus

They had a President because he must enforce established laws
   passed by the Congress of these United States,
An independent Supreme Court to settle problems of all sorts
   among the people in this new land.

Chorus

To pass the laws, they did create a congress to facilitate
   the rightful needs and wishes of the people.
Two legislative bodies for Congressmen and Senators
   to pass the statues in this new land.

Chorus

And for our freedoms to preserve, a Bill of Rights designed to serve
   to guarantee the freedoms of the people.
No government could take away our right to speak and meet and pray
   or guard our families in this new land.

Chorus

This nation ne'er would have a king; A monarchy could only bring
   excesses caused by independent power.
A president they would elect with a sworn duty to protect
   the Constitution of this new land.

Chorus

Abraham Lincoln

THE CIVIL WAR

Words & Music by Fred Cooper

The Civil War started in 1861.
    The North and the South faced each other with a gun.
They fought for four long years through snow and summer's heat.
    In 1865, the South faced its defeat.

Chorus

And the War raged on
    furious as could be
Six-Hundred thousand soldiers died,
    a tragic victory.

The Union states were in the North,
    Confederates in the South.
One issue then was slavery;
    Of that there was no doubt.
The South said that slavery had always been their way.
    The North said "No, no man should be another person's slave."

Still others said the issue was a state's authority;
    To say what should be right or wrong within their boundaries.
Could the nation force its will against a state's own sovereignty?
    Or could a state secede and break the nation's unity?

Chorus

Abe Lincoln was the President of the Union states.
    Jeff Davis led the South in those years of strife and hate.
Ulysees S. Grant was Northern General in Chief.
    Confederate Commander was Robert E. Lee.

In South Carolina down in Charleston Bay, Ft. Sumter fell to Southern troops
    the war was under way.
The Southern boys took over that island fortress then
    and held it 'till the war was almost at its end.

Chorus

The Civil War

In Virginia at Manassas, the first Battle of Bull Run,
  The South and North collided, but the Southern army won.
It gave the South much confidence, they thought that they could win.
  It made the War much longer than it would have ever been.

The North had lots of factories for guns and ships and shells.
  The South relied on money crops, tobacco, cotton bales.
The Confederates sent to Europe for the armaments of war,
  But when the Union blocked their ports, the South received no more.

Chorus

Not only was it fought on land, but also on the sea.
  The South owned the Merrimac, it fought ingeniously.
It clashed with the Monitor, that frigate of the North.
  Those ironclad vessels changed the course of Naval war.

In '62, the Union charged the capital of the South
  to cut the railroad lines and knock their major armies out.
Confederate army soldiers held their capital that day;
  But lost some major battles in old Virgin-i-a.

Chorus

The Shenandoah Valley was the path through which they surged
  To a town in Pennsylvania by the name of Gettysburg.
Lee's troops were devastated, were forced into retreat.
  It turned the tide against the South in July of '63.

On the Mississippi River, the Union troops attacked
  To stop the Southern armies and split the South in half.
They captured ol' New Orleans and finally Vicksburg,
  And after that, the South was practically deterred.

Chorus

The Civil War

Bull Run and Antietam, Cold Harbor, Fredericksburg,
  Perryville and Nashville, Stone Harbor and Vicksburg,
Chattanooga, Chickamauga, Shiloh, Mobile Bay,
  were the names of famous battles in our nation's darkest day.

In the final year of war, Grant fought furiously;
  He captured Virginia and finally Tennessee.
In the state of Alabama, he captured Mobile Bay,
  And when he routed Nashville, the end was on its way.

Chorus

In the Battle of Atlanta, Gen'ral Sherman with his might,
  Destroyed that Southern city, ravaged everything in sight.
He marched on to Savannah, burning cities, fields, and inns.
  That's why they say that Georgia, then, was gone with the wind.

When Grant captured Richmond in 1865,
  The Southern troops were finished; Lee could not survive.
At a place called Appomattox in Virginia, one day,
  The Confederacy surrendered, and the South was held at bay.

Chorus

Reconstruction

Words & Music by Fred Cooper

Verse

When the Ci - vil War was o - ver in eight - teen six - ty five, the un - ion was di - vid - ed, the south did not sur - vive. Re - con - struc - tion was the pro - cess to re - u - nite the states that free - dom law and jus - tice might a - gain - per - pet - u - ate.

Chorus

Re - con - struc - tion af - ter the Ci - vil War when the states were re - u - ni - ted and the south would rise no more.

When the Civil War was over in 1865,
   The Union was divided, the South did not survive.
Reconstruction was the process to reunite the states
   that freedom, law and justice might again perpetuate.

Chorus

Reconstruction, after the Civil War,
   when the states were reunited and the South would rise no more.

Reconstruction started in 1865.
   The process took twelve years, though few were satisfied.
By 1877, the process found its end
   when th' eleven Southern states were all admitted once again.

In '63, Lincoln had a plan he would enact,
   said the South was in rebellion, but their statehood was intact.
He proposed an oath of loyalty for 10 percent or more,
   declared that when this number signed, their rights would be restored.

Chorus

The Republicans in Congress were angry with this plan,
   Felt the South should be well punished for their having left the land.
They wanted them considered as foreign, conquered states who would
   have to do much more before they could repatriate.

On the 14th day of April in 1865,
   Lincoln, then, was murdered and his plan did not survive.
Andrew Johnson became President, and it was his to guide
   this nation through those years when very few were satisfied.

Chorus

Well the Northern states survived the war with property intact,
   but the South had been destroyed by Union armies' fierce attack.
Cities, railroads, houses, crops and factories were void.
   The economy and government were totally destroyed.

The biggest change of all was that the slaves, at last, were free.
　　They left the old plantations to experience liberty.
But they had no jobs or property to support them or their kin.
　　Former masters had no money to employ them once again.

Chorus

The Freedmen's Bureau formed to aid the devastated South
　　started hospitals and schools, and handed food and clothing out.
It also had a court system to handle those disputes
　　'tween former slaves and masters, true justice to impute.

Andrew Johnson re-established Southern governments just when
　　the Confed'rates agreed to swear allegiance once again.
The power was returned to white planters as before,
　　former slaves were still oppressed in this newly caused uproar.

Chorus

Well Congress overturned Johnson's Reconstruction plan.
　　They refused to accept the new Southern congressmen.
Passed the Fourteenth Amendment to grant equal rights and votes
　　to blacks as well as whites and to all the common folk.

The Republican Congress passed the Reconstruction Acts
　　which abolished Southern rule formed under Andrew Johnson's pacts.
They registered black voters and formed mixed governments.
　　The Congress controlled everything which was their full intent.

Chorus

The Congress of the Northern States was firmly in control.
　　They commanded Southern states new constitutions to unfold.
They sent the Northern army to enforce their stricter laws.
　　A social revolution in the South it surely caused.

Reconstruction

This new day in the South seemed too good to survive.
  Blacks and whites in government walked truly side by side.
Black mayors, legislators, teachers, congressmen,
  had rights they'd never dreamed of when they'd been the slaves of men.

Chorus

The carpetbaggers came to take advantage of the South.
  Politicians, teachers, businessmen who the Northern cause espoused.
They set up southern governments that were friendly to the North.
  They were hated by the South who tried to throw them out by force.

Racial violence increased throughout the angry Southern lands.
  They formed their white militias such as the Ku Klux Klan.
They used Intimidation to prevent the new black vote.
  It took lots of Northern arms to keep those governments afloat.

Chorus

In '69, the Fifteenth Amendment was in place.
  States could not deny the right to vote because of race.
This was the most important of the Reconstruction's laws.
  It formed the base of Civil Rights in future freedoms' cause.

The cost of reconstruction was a burden to the North.
  Supporting occupation armies was a most expensive course.
In 1876, Southern home rule was returned
  the vic'tries of the last ten years were gone to all concerned.

Chorus

Reconstruction was a failure almost from the start.
  The benefits of freedom, they just could not impart.
But men must keep on trying always through the years,
  to erase hate and injustice and wipe away the tears.

Chorus

Go West Young Man

Words & Music by Fred Cooper

When the U - ni - ted States was born   there were   thir- teen   states   o - ver

on   the   great   At - lan - tic   o - cean   shore.   There   was   a

great   ex - panse   yet   to   cul - ti - vate   o - ver

at   this   brand   new   na - tion's   west - ern   door.   Go

west   young   man   to   a   bright   and   shin - ing   land.   You   will

find   a   brand   new   start   with   a   song   u - pon   your   heart.   Per - se -

ver - ance   is   the   key   as   you   live   ex - pec - tant - ly   in   a

land   of   gold - en   op - por - tu - ni - ty.

When the United States was born, there were thirteen states
    gathered on the great Atlantic Ocean shore.
There was a great expanse yet to cultivate over at this
    brand new nation's western door.

These lands were claimed by England, France and Spain,
    but were occupied by Indian nation tribes.
A land of forests, rivers, deserts, mountains and the western plains
    where the buffalo and wild life once did thrive.

Chorus

Go west, young man, to a bright and shining land.
    You will find a brand new start with a song upon your heart.
Perseverance is the key, as you live expectantly,
    in this land of golden opportunity.

When they spoke of the West in those early days,
    They meant Kentucky, Indiana, Tennessee.
Pioneers like Daniel Boone blazed a wilderness trail
    Thro' the lands of tribal Indians and trees.

The Northwest Territory was a conquest grand
    Of the Revolutionary War.
Ohio, Indiana, Illinois and Michigan
    Was the farthest west that men had gone before.

Chorus

Congress passed the Northwest Ordinance Act
    Before the 1800's had begun.
It ensured that governments of these vast new lands
    By U.S. law and justice would be run.

In the year eighteen four, an expedition was sent out
    To explore those uncharted western lands.
They sailed the rivers, crossed the mountains where the Indians did roam
    Till they reached the great Pacific Ocean sands.

Chorus

Louisiana was a land that was owned by France.
    They received it in a treaty made with Spain
The Mississippi River ran along that great expanse.
    It was the highway for our produce and our grain.

From the Mississippi River on the Eastern side
    To the slopes of Rocky Mountains' eastern face.
From New Orleans to Canada, a giant land.
    Fifteen states would later occupy this space.

Chorus

Napoleon was the ruler of land of France,
    And to conquer Europe was his major goal.
So he sold Louisiana back in eighteen three
    For the money that would furnish his bankroll.

Florida was owned by the land of Spain.
    It was a land of warlike Indians and thieves.
It was a base where hostile forces could attack our states
    And a problem that our leaders must relieve.

Chorus

In 1819, our Congress made a deal
    And it bought the territory back from Spain.
It secured our southern border with U.S. control
    And restored some law and order once again.

Well, the southwest part of this vast and spacious land
    Was owned by the king and queen of Spain.
Including California, Texas from the mighty Rio Grande
    To the mountains and the western desert plains.

Chorus

Mexico took over back in 1821
    When the Spaniards were defeated and expelled.
They feared the Texans would take over just as they had done,
    so they tried these brand new settlers to repel.

The Texas Revolution came in 1836
    At the Alamo where Texans nobly died.
But their struggles were avenged on the San Jacinto plains
    Where the fledgling Texas Army turned the tide.

Chorus

The importance of this battle, do not underestimate.
    The impact of the conflict must be known.
For it meant that all or portions of the western states,
    The United States would ultimately own.

When Texas joined the Union back in 1845,
    A new conflict with Mexico began.
Mexico did claim much of Texas property,
    And said the border was not the Rio Grande.

Chorus

War was declared back in 1846.
    And the battles did continue two long years.
In the treaty, on the map, California and Utah,
    Arizona and Nevada did appear.

With the Gadsden Purchase in 1853,
    the southern border took its final shape.
We bought that strip of land so a railroad one day might be able to
    cross the southern states.

Chorus

The northwest lands in those early Western days
    Were by England and the U.S. jointly shared.
But after settlers headed West on the Oregon Trail,
    A negotiated border was prepared.

That, my friend, tells the story how the West was won
    In the eighteenth and the nineteenth century.
How Americans conquered this great expanse
    And established it from sea to shining sea.

Chorus

Early American Railroad

The Transcontinental Railroad

Words & Music by Fred Cooper

Oh, once this nation was an untamed land
   East and West were divided by a mighty span
Full of mountains and prairies where the wild wind blows,
   Then the country started growin' where the railroad goes.

Chorus

Where the railroad goes, where the railroad goes;
   America is growin' where the railroad goes.

They struck gold in California in 1849;
   Men rushed to the West to seek their fortunes in the mines.
But they had to go through Panama or clear around Cape Horn
   Or they scaled the mighty mountains and the deserts full of thorns.

Chorus

Well, their journey was a long one full of terrible travails.
   Some died in stormy shipwrecks or on steamy jungle trails.
The ones who crossed the country in those wild West days
   Faced heat and cold and suffering, even Indian raids.

Chorus

In '61, the Civil War had only just begun;
   California was a new state and a prize to be won;
The Pacific Railroad Act was passed in order to ensure
   California's Union loyalty would certainly endure.

Chorus

Back west in California, the wealth increased.
   They opened trade with China and the great Far East.
They grew crops and dug min'rals, copper, ores, and gold
   But they needed iron rails so the goods could be sold.

Chorus

The planning for the project was the greatest of its time;
   Locomotives from New York, iron rails from eastern mines;
To ship around the continents took more than half a year
   before they could arrive on San Francisco's pier.

Chorus

The Central Pacific started from the west;
   Began in Sacramento, faced a tough and mighty test;
The Union Pacific was their rival in the east;
   From Omaha, they laid the rails, the labor never ceased.

Chorus

The obstacles they faced were far too great to be ignored,
   To cross the rugged mountains and the mighty rivers ford.
They built across the deserts and the prairies of the plains,
   Fought heat and cold and Indians o'er the vast terrains.

Chorus

They chipped out mountain tunnels and fought burning desert heat.
   Iron men against exposure, even buffalo stampedes.
They were farmers, miners, convicts, crooked gamblers and more,
   And veterans from North and South who'd fought the Civil War.

Chorus

The corruption with the money was a story to be told
   Robber baron crooks lined their pockets full of gold.
There were Senators and Congressmen impeached and vilified,
   But that didn't stop the railroad as it crossed the Great Divide.

Chorus

In the West, the railroad workers deserted to the mines
    So they hired Chinese laborers who got there just in time.
From the East, they hired Irishmen, who'd traveled to the states,
    To seek out wealth and fortune and improve their low estates.

Chorus

For the Indians, the railroad was a tragedy at hand.
    The white man crossed their hunting grounds and drove them from their land.
They knew their ancient way of life was coming to a close,
    For progress caused injustice and uncounted human woes.

Chorus

Alongside railroad work camps sprung up little Wild West towns.
    Drunken swindlers and con men, and gamblers all around.
They took the workers' money with their schemes and crooked deals.
    That's why those little shanty towns were called "hell on wheels."

Chorus

After seven years of toil and sweat, through blist'ring heat and cold,
    At Promontory, Utah, they drove that spike of gold.
The people of America were feelin' oh, so fine;
    They'd accomplished the impossible in 1869.

Chorus